Mill City Press, Inc.

Mill City Press, Inc.
212 3rd Avenue North, Suite 570
Minneapolis, MN 55401
1.888.MILLCITY
www.millcitypress.net

ISBN 13: 978-1-934248-67-6
ISBN 10: 1-934248-67-3
LCCN: 2007938945

Cover Design by James Wilkinson/Dzyn Lab
Interior Design by Andrea Horne

Printed in the United States of America

THE TENNEY QUILT

Celebrating the Women of Minnesota's Tiniest Town

HEIDI HAAGENSON

TABLE OF CONTENTS

INTRODUCTION.. 5

CHAPTER 1 – THE STORY.. 11

CHAPTER 2 – THE TEACHERS............................... 19
- Octavia
- Linna

CHAPTER 3 – THE STOREKEEPERS
AND BUSINESSWOMEN.. 41
- Nellie
- Audrey
- LaVanche

CHAPTER 4 – THE HOME MAKERS....................... 73
- Lizzie
- Gertie

CHAPTER 5 – THE NURSES..................................... 113
- Violet
- Bertha

CHAPTER 6 – THE FACTORY WORKERS............... 133
- Isabelle

CHAPTER 7 – THE SEAMSTRESSES....................... 143
- Marie

APPENDIX... 155
- Where is Tenney?
- Names Appearing on the Tenney Quilt
- Fictional or Literary Characters Appearing on the Tenney Quilt
- The Minnesota Quilt Project
- Dating the Tenney Quilt

INTRODUCTION

A sense of discomfort and uneasiness overtakes me as I stand on the skeleton of what was once the sidewalk that ran in front of the A.N. Larson Store in Tenney, Minnesota. For as long as I have been working on this project to understand the Tenney that existed in 1928, I have had a wrenching desire to see and touch the A.N. Larson Store, the building that served as my grandfather's livelihood and my mother's childhood home.

As my mother and I stand on this overgrown sidewalk, she announces that as a young girl she roller skated on this spot, literally on this very hunk of concrete on which the soles of my Adidas are currently parked. Back and forth along the sidewalk that started at her stoop, young Helen Jo, with pigtail braids flying behind, would skate past the A.N. Larson Store, past the Louie Wittman Garage, past Cliff's Place, past the Winfield Scott home, past the post office, to the church at the end of the block and back, with pal Neppie Iler not far behind.

Now, only a short section of that sidewalk exists, going from nowhere to nowhere. It stands as a guardian of the empty lot on Main Street where the A.N. Larson Store once stood, a collection of broken chunks of concrete and grass, with the grass clearly having gained the upper hand. And the grass isn't looking well.

I think, with a lump in my throat, about a carefree young school girl who was to become my mother, navigating this section of once-smooth concrete on a pair of old strap-on metal roller skates. For heaven's sake, where has this lump in my throat come from, when my mother standing next to me doesn't even have one? Perhaps it's because she already has the picture formed in her memory and that picture isn't particularly pleasant. I have heard her say that there was a time when she was more than ready to leave Tenney, a dying town that had long since seen its best years. I, on the other hand, have not had the benefit of seeing this little town in its prime. The Tenney Quilt has given me an unquenchable thirst to drink in the sights and sounds of Tenney when Tenney was good.

I feel a palpable, gut-wrenching desire to know and touch the A.N. Larson Store. How did it feel to walk into that store? How did it smell? Did Grandpa have a smile on his face for his customers, or a more serious, thoughtful look? How did he greet his customers and what did they chat about? What was amusing to him in the daily course of his work? What did Grandpa wear to the store? Did he respond immediately when Grandma banged on the stove pipe, indicating that it was time to come upstairs for dinner? Or did he dilly dally around a bit? Was he meticulous about the placement of canned goods on the shelves, and were the boots and work gloves lined up by size from small to extra large?

And what was Tenney *really* like in its prime? What was it like to wake up on a Tenney morning? Were dogs barking? Were people milling about on the street? Who were those people, and what activities filled their days? Was piano music wafting through the open door of the Tenney Church in preparation for the Sunday morning worship service? Were there clean clothes flapping in the breeze on Minnie Wittman's clothesline? Was the train whistle blowing? Were there sounds of children playing in the Tenney School yard? Who were the unmistakable personalities that gave Tenney its identity?

I want so badly to see it now and to have Tenney put her arm around my shoulder and share her secrets. All I can conjure up at this point is a broken up old sidewalk, a bunch of dilapidated buildings, a few stories, and some old photographs. And—the Tenney Quilt.

The sidewalk serves no purpose. The building—indeed the entire town—that this sidewalk served is long gone. There are no children in Tenney to roller skate. Its few inhabitants have no knowledge or association with the people who built Tenney from the ground up, danced in the Town Hall and drew their water from the town pump. They cannot even imagine a time when children's voices were heard in the school yard and services were held in the Tenney Church. They did not know A.N. Larson, and never had a beer at Cliff's Place. I suppose I could be grateful that the A.N. Larson building was mercifully demolished before it could suffer the slow but sure degradation that has befallen the rest of Tenney's structures. Instead, I am a little ticked off that it is not where I want it to be.

Tenney stands eerily deserted and lonely today, the wind blowing through town with little to slow its progress. Doors in abandoned buildings hang from one rusty hinge, stuck in a half-open position, causing an occasional creaking sound as the wind accelerates or changes direction. A sway-backed mare that seems to be on the further side of middle age is tethered to a stake in what was once the backyard of the church parsonage, looking up from her afternoon snack with only casual interest. A stray cat emerges cautiously from the building that once housed the Klugman Store. I have a sense that people are looking out of their windows at me. It is way too quiet. This is how it has been for many, many years.

I am torn between a sense of uneasiness and an intense sense of belonging. I want to turn around and run away from the eeriness of it all, and at the same time I want to find a rake and a shovel and make amends with the damage that time, weather, and neglect have created. I take a picture of my mother on that sidewalk. I walk back and forth a few times on an imaginary route between the A.N. Larson Store and the Louie Wittman Garage. I spend some time silently studying that piece of sidewalk, forcing my mind to magically transform the broken pieces of concrete into something that would befit a carefree young girl's roller skating path. Occasionally, I find myself looking up and trying in vain to make the A.N. Larson Store materialize before my eyes.

* * *

Our history as a nation has most often been told by men. In Tenney, Minnesota in the year 1928, a group of women became writers of history as they captured their tiny town through the careful stitching of names onto ***The Tenney Quilt***.

* * *

"Today we are in the midst of an explosion of interest in women's history, and historians, traditionally attracted to the written word as the way of understanding the past, are increasingly recognizing the need to turn to other sources as well, since women, who were often denied education and discouraged from writing, left fewer records than men. One source, and a paramount one, is their quilts. For if comparatively few women wrote, practically all of them sewed, and in their quilts, especially, they found a capacious medium for expression. For vast numbers of women, their needles became their pens and quilts their eminently expressive texts."

Hearts and Hands, Ferrero, Hedges and Silber

CHAPTER 1

- The Story -

The Tenney Quilt has been in my family since it was created in 1928 in the village of Tenney, Minnesota, a little Red River Valley town on the Minnesota-North Dakota border. Frankly, you probably have not had the occasion to visit Tenney—at least on purpose.

I joke, as my father and many others have, about the current population of Tenney, applying modern demographic measures to a town with a grand total of six citizens. Indeed, one death, one birth, one retirement essentially modifies the demographics by the largest percentage in the history of modern municipal recordkeeping. One can read various accounts of Tenney having the highest average age in the United States. A murder in the town, when Tenney boasted a population of four citizens, gave Tenney the distinction of having the highest murder rate, per capita, in the United States. And it may sound downright impressive that the town's population increased by 50% during the 1990s. That is, until one realizes that two people moved in to town. As it turns out, the population grew from four to six.

This sad skeleton of a once-thriving western Minnesota railroad town has a rich local history, full of people whose stories are worth telling. Lives began, lives were lived, and lives ended. Some stayed because they loved it as their home town, some couldn't wait to leave, and some returned to Tenney as their final resting place. The little village produced nurses, teachers and factory workers. Musicians, bums, storekeepers, doctors, farmers, and railroad workers have called Tenney their home town. My great grandmother, grandmother, and mother grew up here. They were a part of Tenney, and Tenney was a part of them, and thus the pulse of Tenney courses through my blood. Tenney's people were colorful, hard-working German immigrants.

Set aside the Wheaton-Dumont Cooperative Elevator, and there is not one residential, commercial, or community building in Tenney that is currently in a usable state, at least by most people's standards. The town's six aforementioned residents live in mobile homes or homes that seem to struggle to stand up. You have to give these folks credit. They have dreams of restoring the town to some semblance of small town splendor, but so far it seems to have remained in the dream stage. Given this state of affairs, one cannot help but enjoy pondering the scene on a Saturday evening in 1928 as neighboring farmers and their families arrived in town, freshly bathed, with the men gathering at "Cliff's Place" to drink three-two beer and play pool, and the women congregating at the A.N. Larson Store to purchase their provisions for the week, sit around the coal-burning stove in the ice cream chairs and catch up on each others' lives. Cars lined the main street—well, OK, the *only* street to speak of—in celebration of this weekly social ritual. Children sought out their friends and continued games begun in the schoolyard such as "Steal the Bacon," "Hopscotch," "Beckon, Beckon," "The Flying Dutchman," and "Blind Man's Bluff." Being within yelling distance of their parents would not have been an issue in Tenney in 1928—nor is it now.

Amid the pool hall sounds spilling out into the evening air may have been the sound of Russell O'Laughlin pounding the piano keys, honky tonk style, on the O'Laughlin porch across the street from the pool hall. In its wheat farming, stock shipping, turn-of-the-century heyday, the village of Tenney boasted one hundred and twenty people. Some sources say two hundred people but that, quite frankly, is a bit of a stretch. Those and a host of others who lived in the surrounding area formed the colorful social network that defined Tenney. By 1928, when the quilt was made, Tenney had already started its decline. The 1930 census recorded only about 60 people living within the confines of the village.

One might argue that it would be best to put this little two-square-block village out of its misery once and for all and turn it into a sugar beet field. So has been the fate of many of the small settlements and farm sites in the surrounding area. As sad as that may seem, the chances of that happening, I suppose, are fairly good in the next few decades. So how do we, then, make sure that the stories of the Tenney people are preserved in order to remember and honor their lives and the little town they called home?

The unlikely instigators are the women of Tenney who, in 1928, created a quilt to raise money to help buy a stove for the Town Hall. Little did these women know the role their benevolence would play in preserving the history of their town.

With the exception of the Tenney School, the Town Hall was the largest building in Tenney, built in 1913 at a cost of $3,490—a hefty price tag in those days. It was built on the main thoroughfare, just next to the town pump, the town's only source of water. Now understand that, when I say *main thoroughfare,* I am talking about a street one block in length. The Town Hall boasted a fine dance floor, a stage with a curtain that displayed advertisements for local businesses and in later years, a balcony across the back. School programs, ice cream and pie socials, basketball games, roller skating outings, theatrical productions, musical performances, 4H meetings, dances, election activities, wedding receptions, and a multitude of other civic and social gatherings occurred in this important place.

When the Town Hall was in need of a cook stove to service the many social events that occurred there, the city coffers were not adequate to purchase such a luxury item. With a stove at the Town Hall, meals could be cooked on site rather than solely in the kitchens of the women who provided them. A project was conceived in which the women of the village would create a "signature quilt," then auction or raffle it off in order to raise money to buy this stove.

Funds were raised in two ways. First, for the price of one dime, any person in Tenney or the surrounding area could reserve a place on the quilt to put his or her signature, to be preserved for the ages. The person signed a quilt block, and the signature was then embroidered onto the fabric. Once it was completed, the quilt generated additional funds through a raffle or possibly an auction. It is not clear exactly how the quilt finally came to rest in the hands of my great aunt LaVanche, particularly since she was the person who apparently coordinated this ambitious project. However, it is my guess that, being a very independent, professional 29-year-old unmarried woman with the means to do so, dear LaVanche bid the highest amount at an auction for the quilt in order to help her beloved Tenney, as well as to retain what would have been a unique and special item representing the home town that she loved.

In some cases a signer actually signed his or her name on a designated piece of fabric and embroidered over the signature. In other cases, it is obvious that the "signer" simply paid the ten cents and handed it over to someone who embroidered large numbers of names. On the quilt, the names appear in groups of five, with four groups of five in one block, for a total of twenty names in each of 35 blocks. The 20 names in each block are presented in a design which leaves a blank spot in the middle. Filling that middle spot of each block is a simple, embroidered floral or floral basket design, done in the typical "redwork" style of the era. The quilt is made of white muslin, front and back, with a blue border on two ends, and blue embroidery thread used to sew the names.

In the center of the quilt is a large square embroidered with the name of "Larson General Store." By its very nature as a grocery, dry goods store and, at various points in the history of Tenney, the post office, the Larson General Store was the center of activity in town. So it is perhaps appropriate that the Larson General Store retains the center position on the quilt. Adolph Nathaniel "A.N." Larson, my grandfather, was the proprietor of the Larson General Store. The second floor of that store was the childhood home of my mother; hence, the kinship I feel with this quilt. My grandfather probably would have paid two dollars for that spot on the quilt, representing the amount of money that would have been collected for the number of signatures—twenty—that would have filled that amount of space on the quilt.

The oral history of this quilt indicates that the big black cook stove that sat in the Town Hall for many years was most likely the stove that was purchased with the proceeds of this quilt. Old timers remember that stove, on which the Tenney women created many, many meals and which probably remained in the Town Hall until the building's roof began to collapse and the building demolished, for safety's sake, in the late 1980s.

In all, there are 700 "signatures" on the quilt; however, it should be noted that some Tennyites purchased multiple spots and their names therefore appear more than once. John Peter Polifka, my great grandfather, leads the pack with eight appearances. John Polifka was 61 years old in 1928 when the quilt was made. Jack O'Laughlin, a prominent citizen in Tenney as owner and manager of the local Farmers Elevator, purchased seven spots. Jack and his wife Rose, one of the few Irish Catholic families in town, also had the distinction of having the only home in town with running water at one time. In all, there are 530 separate people represented on the Tenney Quilt.

In addition to these Tenney area people, the quilt contains the names of fictional and literary character names, as well as a few business names. These fictional names alone provide a fascinating view into the times. They shed light on the nursery rhymes children were chanting and the literature that was being taught and recited in the Tenney School or being read by the masses. Among the many nursery rhyme characters are, for example, Old King Cole, Jack and Jill, Miss Muffet, and Bo-Peep. British literary characters seem to prevail among the remaining fictional signatures: Gunga Din, Lady Macbeth, Scrooge, Silas Marner, and Maggie Tuliver, for example. A complete listing and description of these fictional names appears in the Appendix.

Among the names appearing on the quilt are my maternal grandmother and grandfather, great grandmother and grandfather, and an assortment of great aunts and uncles and other shirttail relatives or people related through marriage. Several of these are people that have been important in my life, particularly my grandmother, Audrey Polifka Larson, who was married to A.N. Larson of the Larson General Store. As one of her only three grandchildren, I grew up very close to my dear "Grandma Aud," who passed away in 1999 at the age of 95. Her sister, LaVanche Polifka Gill, also appears on the quilt and was the original owner of this treasure. LaVanche was as close to being my grandma as a person can be without being one. To know Grandma Aud and LaVanche both had a hand, quite literally, in creating this quilt and, in fact, ran their fingers over its surface many times over the years makes it special to me personally. They spoke of Tenney and its people frequently. Tenney was their home. Tenney was "the good ol' days." Oh how I wish I would have listened more closely to those stories.

Beyond its sentimental value to me personally, the quilt's value to a wider audience lies in its historical significance. And the historical significance of this quilt seems even greater when one considers that the village of Tenney, for all practical purposes, has ceased to exist. The quilt ties together 530 separate lives to one small village and one year in history. That village is Tenney, and the year is 1928. As has been the case in so many small towns in the Red River Valley, corporate farming operations have gradually purchased much of the surrounding land and razed the farm houses and homesteads where my mother played as a child. Shells of the school house, the Social Hall, the Tenney Church, and the old fire hall still stand, as well as a few uninhabited homes. But most other buildings have either been destroyed or stand dilapidated and empty. My great grandmother's house which I visited many times as a child was finally bulldozed several years ago, unable any longer to bear the weight of decades of Minnesota winters, steadily declining care, and a town that seemingly no longer justified its existence. The A.N. Larson General Store, the pool hall, the bank, the post office and the Town Hall—all important buildings that were the backbone of the town in 1928—are gone. Tenney now has the distinction of being the smallest town in the State of Minnesota. The significance of the Tenney Quilt lies in its documentation of the people of Tenney and what Tenney *once was,* when all these buildings stood tall and served as the epicenter of many lives. The purpose of the quilt—to purchase a cook stove for the town hall—tells volumes about what was important to Tenney's women: food, friendship, fellowship, support for others, and service to community. Sociability was one of the primary expressions of German American ethnicity (Conzen, 2003).

So, there is a quilt that sits in a glass bookcase in my home—a quilt with 700 names, a decorative, visual response to the lives and values of the women of Tenney, but also a historical document representing the social structure of the village of Tenney and the surrounding area as it existed in 1928. The entrusting of this quilt from one generation to the next—to the next—begs that someone along the way tells the stories of these Tenney women. I heard the begging.

I could have chosen to write a historical account of Tenney, or about the influential men and women who lived there, or Tenney's contribution to the history of Wilkin County. Instead, I chose to let the Tenney quilt, through its embroidered names, coax me to learn more about those names, particularly the women. Each name has a story. So often it is the stories of men that we read about in history books. The stories of women are difficult to trace, as their lives were often not considered as remarkable as those of their men. Once married, a woman took the name of her husband and her own first name disappeared and became "Mrs.". If she had a career when she was single, she often discontinued it after marriage, in accordance with the societal expectation that she stay home, raise children, and defer all family successes to the man of the house.

These women, though long departed, have become my friends. Most I never knew. Some left Tenney with a sense of adventure and optimism, only to have lives filled with hardship. Some lived most of their lives in Tenney, leaving as old people only when Tenney was no longer able to take care of them, or perhaps they died there. Some drifted in to Tenney, stayed awhile, and drifted out. And some Tenney youngsters set out in the world to find a better life and never looked back.

I have chosen to tell the stories of those women whose names begged for a story. Most of these names reflect the German heritage predominant in the Tenney area: Linna Gordhamer, Violet Gillaspey, Bertha Berry, Audrey and LaVanche Polifka, Lizzie Strobusch, and Gertie Kapitan. But I could not resist Octavia Askegaard, of Norwegian heritage, or the Scottish girls, Nellie Dalgarno, Isabelle Dalgarno and Marie Hadwick. Their stories are all intertwined in some way with the little Minnesota town where my mother sat on the front step of the A.N. Larson Store and watched the world go by.

CHAPTER 2

- *The Teachers* -

Octavia

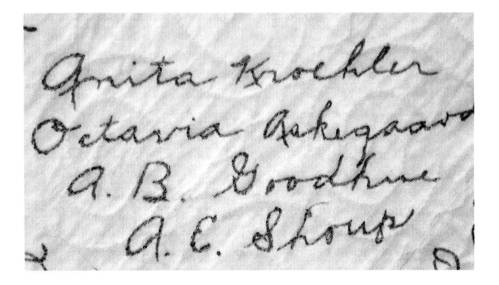

Octavia Askegaard was a person whose story I knew I would tell, just having read this Nordic-sounding name that was seemingly attached to no one else on the quilt. It was a name that seemed somewhat of an oddity in the German stronghold of Tenney, Minnesota. I had to know more.

In August, 1928, as the quilt project was in full swing, Octavia, known as "Ocky" to her friends and family, had just arrived on the scene in Tenney as an 18-year-old graduate of the two-year "intermediate" teaching program at Moorhead State Normal School. Having been born into a family of teachers and being an independent, fun-loving, intelligent girl, Ocky was ready to take on the children of Tenney.

Coming from the small village of Comstock only 40 miles north, she must have felt a certain sense of comfort and familiarity as she arrived in this little prairie town of Tenney. One can only imagine the excitement, but also the anxiety and fear, that a young 18-year-old girl might feel in such a situation. Octavia's fortitude was perhaps girded by the concurrent arrival of Miss Janice Johnson of Virginia, Minnesota, also new to Tenney and the Tenney School. Together they made up the entire faculty, with Ocky teaching the primary grades and Janice in "the grammar room," taking care of grades five through eight. Try to imagine the entire educational system in Tenney in the hands of two 18-year-old girls!

The Tenney School, or "District 30" as it was known, was organized as a result of a petition granted in 1887 to 24 Campbell Township residents. It began as a one-room wood frame schoolhouse in one corner of town, which stood for 21 years until a larger brick school house was built in a different corner of town. Initially, there were three teachers in the brick school, as the years surrounding the turn of the century were Tenney's peak population years. That brick school stood proudly for the children of Tenney until 1956, when Irene Doyle and Doris Raguse served as its two teachers. It was then closed and the children were sent to the neighboring town of Campbell. The school building was subsequently sold to Russell (Red) O'Laughlin, who ran the Farmers' Elevator in town at the time, and used the school building for storing grain! Perhaps it is my love of education, as well as my sentimentality for the town of Tenney and its history that makes this difficult for me to swallow. The thought of busting a hole in the roof and dumping grain into the classrooms of a grand old building such as the Tenney School makes me sad, if not downright angry.

The brick schoolhouse stood for 50 more years, until 2006, when one of my several visits to Tenney revealed a building that had finally fallen into itself. Before that time, the roof had caved in, but the building itself had managed to remain standing, though struggling to maintain its dignity. The Tenney School, once the proudest building in town and a building that outlasted most, now shares the same fate as the town's other major structures. Just like the sidewalk in front of the A.N. Larson Store, the school sidewalk, today, leads to nowhere. A pile of bricks and debris now marks the spot where the voices of children were once heard reciting their letters, numbers, and Thanksgiving program pieces.

Ocky, born in 1909, was the second oldest of eight children of Oscar and Annie Askegaard, both teachers. Coming from a family of ten, Ocky was no stranger to child management. There was no full high school program at Comstock High School until 1929 so, at age 16, having gone as far as she could in Comstock, Ocky began her two-year "intermediate" teacher training program at the Moorhead Normal School. According to information obtained from the Normal School yearbook that year, Ocky was involved in Pi Mu Phi, Moorhead's first sorority, and a variety of other clubs and social groups such as the Country Life Club, Chorus, CampFire, and W.A.L. (Women's Athletic League). By all accounts, it appeared as though Octavia was an intelligent, energetic, talented young woman with lots of interests.

Moorhead Normal School offered free tuition to those students who signed a declaration intending to teach in Minnesota at least two years following graduation. Tuition would otherwise have been $20 per quarter. Board and room at the College was $25 per month (MN State Univ Moorhead, 2007). So, given that Ocky would most likely have signed the declaration, and with a few other miscellaneous fees added, would have paid somewhere between $64 and $84 per quarter to obtain her teaching training. The final teaching credential would come with the passage of the Minnesota State Board Examinations. Sample questions from the 1926 exam, only two years before Octavia would have taken such an exam, are as follows:

- A cow eats 38 pounds of ensilage each day. How many days will the contents of a silo 12 feet in diameter and 28 feet high last a herd of 15 cows if one cubic foot of ensilage weighs 40 pounds?

- Find the cost of plowing a field 360 rods by 180 rods at $1.50 an acre. Then find the distance around the field.

- State two ways in which the Constitution of the United States differed from the Articles of Confederation.

• Mention a distinguished American connected with each of two of the following: League of Nations, Construction of the Panama Canal, Conservation of Forests, The World Court, The Disarmament Conference.

It is interesting to note the transformation that occurred in Ocky in her two years away at college. Her first-year photograph shows a tentative, reserved, 16-year-old, fresh from her humble little northern Wilkin County town of Comstock. In 1928, her second year at the college, she has blossomed into what appears to be a happy, confident, stylish, sociable young woman ready to conquer the world. School teachers' looks had changed considerably in these years with the advent of the permanent wave method of hair styling in 1926 (Miller, 1998), along with an increasingly modern style of dress. Ocky clearly followed the latest trend in hair style, arriving at her college with a straight, short, simple hair style and leaving with a stylish, sophisticated permanent wave. This second photograph was taken the very year she began her teaching career in Tenney—the year the quilt was created.

Octavia and Janice, having come to Tenney in August of 1928, roomed initially with Toby and Mary Tyler and their two young chil-

Octavia at age 18, her first year at the Tenney School

dren. Later that fall, the two young teachers were forced to find another home as the Tylers moved out of Tenney when Toby found employment at a garage in Wheaton. Gust and Ida Klugman, proprietors of the Klugman Store in Tenney, took them in. Octavia grew to love the Klugmans and would remain friends with the family for many years.

Octavia's predecessor in the primary grades of the Tenney School was Miss Myrtle Peterson, who had departed at the end of the previous school year due to her marriage to a Mr. Benson. Many men and women of the time believed that, if a woman had not found a man by age 18 to 20 or thereabouts, she was no good, and certainly by age 25, there was little hope. At that point, the woman could be the subject of mockery, pity, or both. In 1928 most women, whether married or not, were dependent upon the men in their families for financial support. Many teachers, however, remained unmarried for longer periods of time, dedicating their time and resources to their school children. Indeed our Tenney schoolteacher, Octavia, would later be considered an "old maid," not uncommon among her ranks. Octavia would reach the ripe old age of 39 by the time she finally married. Young female teachers supported themselves and often helped other family members. Because their teaching contracts often included room and board, some teachers did have a certain amount of disposable income, even during hard times, to send to their families.

Young women such as Octavia serving as the community's school teachers were provided with many social opportunities, and it is not surprising that they would want to take part in the social life of the community given the fact that they were hardly adults themselves. As 18- to 20-year-olds, Octavia and Janice joined in the social activities of the young people in town, including 24-year-old Audrey Polifka, who would one day be my grandmother. Octavia at times hiked with other young women in town to one of the neighboring towns to go to a moving picture, or caught a ride to Breckenridge, the county seat, to take care of school business or to go shopping. And, of course the Town Hall in Tenney provided many social opportunities such as pie socials and dances for the young teachers to meet and get to know all the local bachelors. School boards sometimes made schoolteacher selections based on appearance, from photographs sent to them in advance. I don't know if Wilkin County used such a method but if they did, Ocky could certainly have passed such judgment as her photograph showed a seemingly happy, vibrant young woman.

However, despite all of the opportunities for social engagement, teachers were expected to be role models for their school children, both in school and out. A teacher contract from a Wisconsin school in 1922 lists the following expectations of female teachers:

- May not get married (contract becomes null and void immediately if this occurs)

- May not have company with men

- Must be home between the hours of 8 p.m. and 6 a.m., unless in attendance at a school function

- May not loiter downtown in ice cream parlors

- May not leave town at any time without the permission of the chairman of the Trustees

- May not smoke cigarettes

- May not drink beer, wine, or whiskey

- May not ride in a carriage or automobile with any man except her father or brother

- May not dress in bright colors

- May not dye her hair

- Must wear at least two petticoats

- May not wear dresses more than 2 inches above the ankles

- May not wear face powder, mascara, or paint the lips

- Must sweep the classroom floor at least once daily, scrub the classroom floor at least once weekly with soap and hot water, clean the blackboard at least once daily, and start the fire at 7 a.m. so that the room will be warm at 8 a.m. when the children arrive.

Though these parameters pre-date Octavia's arrival in Tenney by six years, they do shed light on the times in which Octavia and so many other young women in the Midwest were educating children in one- and two-room schoolhouses.

Octavia would have worked ten to twelve hour days, and would have had several chores in addition to teaching students. She would have swept and scrubbed the floors, built a fire in the stove, cleaned the blackboards, and served as jack-of-all trades in the school. She would have met the students at the door to help take off overshoes, coats and caps, and reversed the process in the afternoon. She would have served as mentor, counselor, nurse, mediator, judge, and jury for the students. All of this for approximately $95 per month in Wilkin County during this time period.

Even in the late 1930s when my mother was attending the Tenney School, all water used at the school had to be hauled from the town pump, either by the teacher or sometimes by the older school boys. In Tenney this meant a block-and-a-half hike from the town pump to the school yard. Drinking water was dispensed in the classroom from a crock with a spigot, sitting on a stand with legs. Collapsible tin cups were popular for awhile. Students always brought their own lunches to school in 1928, sometimes carried in a syrup pail. Later on, in the 1930s, my mother remembers bringing a Velveeta Cheese sandwich and canned pear sauce to school every single day in her early school years at the Tenney School. My mother learned the art of canning from her mother, and I loved the home-canned peaches and pears that Mom served during my own childhood.

An important job of the teacher was to dole out discipline to students when needed. The use of a wooden ruler against the knuckles served as a reliable standby for getting a student's attention for punishable behaviors such as whispering, gum chewing, pencil chewing, using the word "ain't," mispronouncing words, throwing a paper wad, or spitting on the school steps or sidewalk. Alternatives to a whack across the knuckles might be a paddling in front of the other students, either by hand or wooden paddle, often while bent over a chair or—gasp!—even the teacher's lap. Some students were known to have worn a sign around their necks announcing "I am a gum chewer." Others were writing "I will not whisper in class" 200 times on the chalkboard. And of course among the most humiliating punishments was for the perpetrator to wear the offending chewing gum on the end of one's nose.

Victor Kath, who was eight years old as our quilt was being unfurled, was 86 years old in 2004 when he told me the story of an incident which occurred when he was in the seventh grade at the Tenney School. The teacher in question was Ida Mae Haagenson who, interestingly, shares my last name. Miss Haagenson was in charge of instructing fourth through eighth graders in Tenney. Victor, who from all reports was a very bright student, sat across the aisle from Frances Klugman, a girl of his own age and with whom he felt a certain degree of annoyance. On this particular school day, Frances arose from her school desk seat and was standing faced toward her desk across the aisle, her backside toward Victor. Some unnamed body part was apparently within reaching distance of 12-year-old pubescent Victor, who could not resist the urge to pinch poor Frances. I did not ask Victor exactly which body part was involved, but I have an idea.

The pinch was apparently enough to inflict a level of discomfort or surprise enough that Frances let out a rather loud squeal. Victor recalls that, after the pinch, Miss Ida Mae Haagenson glared at him for a seemingly endless period of time, apparently pondering her course of disciplinary action. Miss Haagenson then walked over to Victor and slapped him across the face with her hand, leaving a red mark that, according to Victor, remained visible for two weeks. Those two weeks were additionally marked by Victor's banishment from recess. Having been denied recess privileges for two weeks, as well as experiencing the humility of wearing the visible reminder on his face, Victor reports that there were no further pinching incidents. The fact that he remembered this incident that had occurred 74 years prior would indicate that Miss Ida Mae Haagenson made an impression on the young man.

Many times, young female teachers did not last long in any particular school because of the intimidating behavior of the older boys in the class. Meanness and trickery was common, and teachers were often not much older than the oldest students (Dumenil, 1995), so one can only imagine how intimidating some of these strapping young men would have been to an 18- or 19-year-old teacher. Based on her dealings with Victor, Miss Haagenson seemed capable of holding her own.

A school day in the Tenney School, like so many others in 1928, would begin at 9:00 with the school bell ringing; then, once settled, the children would recite the Pledge of Allegiance with their hands over their hearts. Most of us can remember this routine, a wonderful common denominator that linked school-age children across the entire nation, until it became inappropriate, in the eyes of miscellaneous bureaucrats, to declare that we were one nation under God. Children were often greeted in the morning by sayings on the chalk board such as "Honesty is the best policy," or "All that glitters is not gold." Often, before lessons began, a patriotic song or two would be sung.

The day's lessons then began with the learning of letters and numbers among the smaller children, and memory work for the older children, while memories bore the freshness of the morning dew. Memorization and recitations were common at all age levels, either in small groups or individually. The memorization of poetry was particularly common. Given that there were several grade levels in one classroom, it certainly must have been somewhat distracting to the other students who needed to be studying their own lessons. British literature of various sorts was popular in the upper grades in Tenney, as evidenced by the literary figures whose names appear in the Tenney Quilt: Silas Marner, Scrooge, Enoch Arden, Gunga Din, and Lady Macbeth, to name a few. McGuffey readers were used in that time period, and students in the lower grades read Winnie the Pooh.

Fifteen-minute recess periods were held in both the morning and afternoon, with an hour set aside for lunch. No different than today's school children, the Tenney children of 1928 looked forward to their recess time. The school yard in Tenney encompassed a large area in the northwest corner of town, big enough for a game of kitten ball or baseball, or any number of school yard games including "Steal the Bacon," "Andy Over," "Pom Pom Pullaway," or just plain ol' foot races. Though both age 22 the year of the Tenney Quilt, Mae Pithey and Myrtle Polifka were good runners and had been frequent competitors, in earlier days, in schoolyard running races. One balmy winter school day in January, 1929, during Octavia's first school year in Tenney, the teachers and pupils met at 7:30 a.m. at the school with their lunches, and hiked to the Pithey tree claim, where they enjoyed an outdoor winter picnic. They took their time getting back to the school building, continuing their lessons once the wet coats and shoes were removed and put by the stove to dry.

Afternoons at the Tenney School were often the times that the subjects beyond readin', writin' and 'rithmetic were taught—penmanship, etiquette, art, practice for holiday plays and other special events. Penmanship was stressed heavily in the classroom, often using the Palmer method of handwriting. Repetition—repetition—repetition was used to learn and to reinforce good penmanship. Young and old students practiced their penmanship repeatedly on the blackboard or in their tablets as the teacher kept busy with other students. Above average penmanship sometimes opened the door to jobs that otherwise would not have been possible. Clerks, bookkeepers, and census-takers, for example, were known to have excellent penmanship (Felder, 1997). Though there was no high school at the Tenney School, the social training for girls that was taught at the high school level trickled down to the lower grade levels during this time period.

Holidays such as Thanksgiving, Christmas, and Valentines Day became much-anticipated special events in the classroom and spilled out into the community. In 1928, Octavia and Janice and their students put on a Thanksgiving program in the Town Hall which featured "renditions, songs, drills, sketches and a farce." There were 30 children in the Tenney School this year, and each of them had a part in the program. Before Thanksgiving the plays, recitations, one-act plays, and songs were chosen for the upcoming Christmas program, and much time was spent preparing for the big event. Names were drawn for the exchange of Christmas gifts among the school children, and much sport and speculation was involved in keeping the name of the giver secret from the recipient. When the time came, the Town Hall was strung with green and red crepe paper, and a Christmas program was held for all townspeople to attend, whether they had children at the school or not. Kids were washed and scrubbed, hair slicked back or adorned with a ribbon, and they appeared in their Sunday best. After the various performances, coordinated and introduced by Octavia and Janice, someone would slip out the door, dress up as Santa Claus, and re-enter to the sound of sleigh bells. Often there was a bag of candy and an apple for each child. Pupils opened their gifts from their secret givers, receiving items such as pencil boxes, new tablets of paper, or necklaces. The teachers generally received a small gift from each family, and very often the teacher gave something special to each child, such as an Eskimo pie from the Larson Store, or a pencil, and a handmade card.

Valentines Day in 1928 meant an evening Valentines party for the pupils of the grammar room and their teacher, Miss Johnson, at the Polifka home. The evening was spent playing games. At 11:00 p.m. a lunch was served (Don't these Tenney children sleep?), and each child received a treat from the teacher. In the words of the local newspaper, "all reported a fine and dandy time." Earlier in the day, the mothers of the children in Octavia's primary room class were invited to attend school at 3:00. The children put on a program about Lincoln, Washington, and Valentines Day. Why not take care of three holidays all at once? After all the recitations and songs, five-year-old Virginia Dawson passed out a lunch of cake and cocoa which had been prepared by her mother, and each student received a Valentine favor. Then a large box of valentines was distributed. Mothers attending this event were Minnie Wittman, Gertie Kapitan, Ruby Iler, and Minnie and Clara Kath.

During the 1928-29 school year, the school teachers in Tenney organized a box social. Schoolgirls decorated a box which would have, in most cases, been a shoebox that perhaps once held a pair of shoes ordered from the Montgomery Ward catalog. If a shoe box wasn't available, any box would do. The box was then festooned with bows, ribbons, fabric, beads, crepe paper, or any fancy bauble to be found around the house. Once decorated, Mother stepped in, filling the box with cold snacks, hard-boiled eggs, sandwiches, pickles, and perhaps some cornbread or cake. Sometimes the box socials were carried out as auctions, with the decorated, filled boxes auctioned off to the highest bidder and the proceeds used to purchase items needed at school. In this particular case in Tenney the boxes, after the requisite "oohs" and "ahhs," were simply enjoyed by the young girl and her mother or other relative who accompanied her. It was a much anticipated, much celebrated event.

Octavia and Janice formed a "Little Citizens League" at the Tenney School in 1928, in which students not only learned about responsible citizenship, but as "little citizens," had their own jobs to perform during the course of the school day: Victor Kath was the Coaler, David Roach was the Door Tender, Pearl Iler served as the

Eraser Cleaner, Robert Dawson was the Hall Inspector, and Gladys Clark, the Desk Inspector. I am certain that each of these young citizens took their job seriously and was expected to perform their job with the utmost respect and responsibility.

Octavia taught at the Tenney School for three years, leaving the area in the spring of 1931 to take a teaching position in Fergus Falls, a larger town about 20 miles northeast of Tenney and even closer to her home town of Comstock. I suppose it would have to have been considered a great opportunity to move from teaching in a two-room school house to a big "city school."

Many young female teachers of the time got their feet wet in the rural or small town school houses and later moved on to bigger and better things. That is, unless they married, in which case most left teaching entirely. In the 1920s, it was generally accepted that one person—and one person only—in a family could generate a family income. So when a woman married, it was *her* career that was most often surrendered. Love affairs and marriages were sometimes kept secret for this reason. In some locales, teachers were banned outright from being married (Gulliford, 1984). With a limited amount of wage money to distribute, it would not have been considered proper for two people in one family to be bringing in an income when other families would have had none. Gulliford notes, however, that later on during World War II, many of those women who left teaching in order to get married went back to work as teachers under emergency teaching certificates to avert a national education crisis. As in so many other professions, the men were off to war, leaving the education of America's children once again to the women, a trend that continued for decades. In 1926, just two years before the Tenney Quilt, the St. Louis Park Schools (western Minneapolis suburb) fired three teachers simply because they were married (Vaughan, 2002-2003). It was, unfortunately, not unusual.

I have to believe that, even after Octavia left Tenney, the site of her first teaching job and thus her first experience immersing herself in a community as a teacher and role model, Tenney's children and their families remained close to Ocky's heart. I was thrilled to find, when looking through an old scrapbook of my grandmother's, a sympathy card from Octavia Askegaard at the occasion of the tragic death of my uncle in a hunting accident at age 17. And I know that, at least on one occasion—and probably several more—Ocky returned to Tenney for a weekend visit with the Gust Klugman family, with whom she had boarded for one year while teaching at the Tenney School.

Octavia taught in the Fergus Falls School system for several years as an elementary school teacher. This teaching position would prove to be her last when, one day in 1942, Ocky received a flyer in her mailbox soliciting young women, particularly teachers, who were interested in doing something exciting while at the same time helping out the war effort. Octavia, at age 32, had by that time, been teaching for 14 years, and this flyer captured her interest.

Young men and women, but mostly women, were being recruited by the Civil Aeronautics Authority, which would later become the FAA (Federal Aviation Administration). I spoke to George L. Barron, a Navy fighter pilot who worked at the Jamestown, North Dakota Airport as a flight instructor. He told me that Octavia would have spent some time training in Chicago, then would have been assigned to any one of several airports around the country. Trainees, for the three-month course, had to make their way to Chicago, and rent a room for about five dollars per week. The training included standard communications procedures such as pilot-to-ground and vice versa, tower-to-pilot and vice versa, as well as meteorology, appropriate terminology, and the use of the equipment used to make hourly reports of temperature, dew point, wind speed, and cloud height. Additionally, the trainees learned how to prioritize landings and take-offs and how to handle emergencies. This three-month course, which Octavia took during the summer months, qualified her as an "Aircraft Communicator," and upon completion, she was assigned to Jamestown, North Dakota, which had a small air station.

Octavia's job as a radio operator entailed contacting the pilots, observing the weather, and translating the weather into the sequence that gave pilots the weather across the country every hour. She filed flight plans and contacted various locations by teletype. The responsibility of taking charge of 15 to 30 young students in a one-room school house and the accompanying chaotic environment would have been wonderful training for Ocky's position at the airport, in which she calmly and responsibly took care of the needs of pilots from all over the country as constant activity and ticker noise filled the air station. I know that Ocky would have loved the excitement and adventure of this job, and would have been proud to serve her country as a government employee in this way during the war.

During this time that Ocky was working at the Jamestown Airport, her future husband, Kenneth Perry McGregor, was a very successful farmer and livestock trader in Nashua, Iowa. Kenneth, seven years Octavia's senior, had lived his entire life in that community. Back when Octavia was attending her last year at Comstock High School, Kenneth was courting Florence Wilcox in Nashua. Kenneth and Florence were married, and together had had three sons.

As part of his job as a "big time" livestock buyer and seller, Kenneth flew all over the country. He often chartered a plane in Mason City (Iowa) to fly to places such as Chicago, Texas, or further north. Kenneth brought his sons Malcolm and Ronald into his business, and together, the McGregors became major landowners in Chickasaw County, Iowa. They dealt in a variety of livestock including horses, hogs, and cattle, but cattle trading was their primary livelihood. There are many historical references in *The Nashua Reporter*, Nashua's local newspaper, about local people buying teams of horses or cattle from Kenneth, but even more frequently are references to Kenneth's large stock shipments by railroad. At several points during the 1930s, 40s and 50s, Kenneth's stock shipments to the Chicago stockyards were called "the largest stock shipments ever" from the city of Nashua.

Kenneth McGregor was clearly a big businessman with a lot of influence in Nashua. He held several leadership positions within the community. Kenneth was a man who was not afraid to express his opinion or to use his considerable influence as one of the county's major land owners. He served on the school board and on various civic committees, and in organizations in which his three boys were involved such as the Boy Scouts and 4H. He became quite an advocate throughout his adult years for the stringent enforcement of weed eradication laws. His personal crusade to initiate lawsuits against many of his own neighbors for their failure to comply with the weed laws earned him a reputation among some as being argumentative and somewhat domineering. One would have to believe that people both respected him for his business acumen and at the same time resented him for his tendency to occasionally flaunt his status in the region.

Kenneth's wife, Florence, died in 1946. It is curious to me that there appears to be no obituary or mention of her death in *the Nashua Reporter* at any point during that year, nor are there any clues in Kenneth's obituary or in the newspaper about the cause of his wife's death. She clearly had no extended illness, as there were newspaper references in early 1946 about Florence's continuing involvement in various civic and social clubs. Because the investigative reporter in me must know, I was disappointed at my inability to solve this mystery.

The circumstances which brought Octavia together with this man had been a mystery to me until I pieced together the chronicle of Kenneth's life through newspaper accounts in *The Nashua Reporter.* I learned that Jamestown, North Dakota was one of Kenneth's cattle trading destinations. Perhaps it was during one of his flights in to the small air station in Jamestown that Kenneth met Octavia. A possibility of equal credence was that Kenneth's cousin, Borden McGregor, who lived in Jamestown and with whom Kenneth was quite close, may have introduced them.

The same year that Kenneth's first wife Florence died, Kenneth and his cousin Borden worked together on a public sale of 40 registered Herefords at the Jamestown Sales Pavilion. Kenneth made at least two trips by air to Jamestown related to this sale, and I have to believe that one of these trips provided the key to the future of Kenneth and Octavia. I am guessing that either Kenneth met Octavia as she was working at the airport, or that Kenneth's cousin Borden knew of this attractive, intelligent, energetic and *single* women working at the air station, and introduced her to his recently widowed cousin. One can see how Ocky may have been somewhat star struck by this high roller-type who flew across the country, exuded power, owned major parcels of land, and made large business deals. I am sure that Octavia felt this larger-than-life figure was the man of her dreams.

A courtship ensued and Octavia, age 39 and never married, fell in love with the exciting cattle trader from Iowa, and they were married. Kenneth was 45 at the time. Ocky lived the next 28 years of her life as an Iowa farm wife. Kenneth's three sons, at the time of his marriage to Octavia, were ages 21, 18 and 11. Octavia worked her way, to some extent, into the social network of Nashua, becoming active in the First United Methodist Church and social clubs in town. But as was the case with so many women of her time, she never worked outside the home once married. I have to believe that Kenneth was a fervent believer that the man of the house was the provider and a woman's place was to support him in whatever ways he felt proper.

As I had suspected, Octavia did not live a particularly happy life in those years in Nashua. Her nieces have told me she was not lovingly accepted into the family or community in the way that she had perhaps envisioned it. She was an outsider in many ways. When I think of the bright-eyed 18-year-old who bounded in to Tenney in 1928, I am sad for Ocky's later life.

After Kenneth died in 1975, Ocky came full circle, moving back to Minnesota at age 66, and living in an apartment in Moorhead, not far from her extended family. She died a few short years later, in 1980, and is buried next to her father in a little church cemetery outside the village of Comstock, just up the road from little Tenney, Minnesota, where her professional life began.

Linna

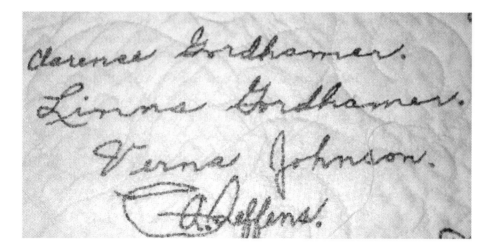

In 1928, Linna Gordhamer was married and living in Brecken-ridge, the county seat, where her husband Clarence was the County Superintendent of Schools. But she was very much at home in Tenney, twenty miles away. Linna was a Tenney girl, born in 1900 to Austin and Alice Pithey. *Pithey* is one of those "Tenney names" that have brought smiles to my family over the years, especially when spoken in the same sentence with the other Tenney classics: Raguse, Polifka, Roach, Glock, Rubish, and Kath, which, by some sort of perversion of modern English language usage, was pronounced "Kates" by those in and around Tenney. I think we can blame my father for initially finding humor and teasing my mother about the names of her youth, and escalating it to Super Bowl status over the years. With Tenney's residents being primarily of German heritage, Johnsons and Petersons were not easy to unearth—though there were a few scattered here and there, and the northeastern part of Wilkin County was primarily Scandinavian.

Reading the names of the women on this quilt for the first time was like opening a treasure chest. I have always been fascinated by

names, and these did not disap-point. Some tickled me more than others: Blanche Funkhouser, Fern Worm, Lizzie Strobusch (pro-nounced "Straw Bush"), Estella Gill, Matilda Lyngaas, Cora Belle Gore, Hermanda Hasse, Isabelle Dalgarno, and my personal favor-ite, Daisy Rose, whose maiden name is even more delightful, Daisy Pithey. My own great aunt's name, LaVanche Polifka, would certainly be on this list had I not had a life-time to become accustomed to the sound of it. And though this book focuses on the women of Tenney, I

Linna (front), sister Daisy, friend "Lundy," and LaVanche Polifka

would be remiss in omitting Fritz Raguse and Winston Roach from the list. They tickle me. And when you consider that Winston's nickname was "Wink"—Wink Roach—well—it just doesn't get any better.

Back to Linna. Linna Vivian Pithey was one of six children, the eldest daughter of Austin and Allie Pithey. The Pitheys were farmers, but farmed just across the railroad tracks from the town site, so practically lived in town. Their pasture served as the town's baseball field at various points in Tenney's history. Linna's future husband, Clarence Morgan Gordhamer, had spent most of his professional life living at home with his parents while working as a school teacher in Kanabec County, Minnesota. The circumstances of Clarence and Linna's original meeting are a mystery to me, but given that both Linna and Clarence once taught in the Tenney School, I have to believe that their paths crossed, either as fellow teachers, or at least as acquaintances while in Tenney. At any rate, Linna, at the age of 24, made her way down the aisle at the Tenney Church with Clarence in 1924. Three years later, Clarence was appointed Wilkin County Superintendent of Schools, a career move that locked them in to the Tenney area for the rest of their lives.

The Records of the Wilkin County Superintendent of Schools indicate that the County Superintendent position was established in 1851 when Minnesota was still a territory. The superintendents were typically elected for two-year terms and were often re-elected term after term. This was the case with Clarence, who served a total of 16 years and would most likely have served longer if not for his untimely death by heart attack at age 53 in 1943. As was the case with young Octavia Askegaard and her contemporaries, single women teachers were often quite isolated in rural or small town schools, and they looked upon their County Superintendents as mentors and advisors. When one considers that these young teachers were expected to set examples for students and their families, be upstanding citizens, and in many cases be leaders in their small communities—all on top of their teaching responsibilities—one begins to realize the value of having the support of a County Superintendent. Linna, after having taught in the classroom, served her husband and the country schools of Wilkin County as Deputy County Superintendent for many years, including the year of the quilt, and in 1943 was named the County

Superintendent when Clarence passed away. When Linna took over in 1943, there were still 80 school districts in the county. Only a few remain today.

In their roles as County Superintendent, Clarence and Linna visited each school a few times each school year. In 1930, when Octavia was still at the Tenney School, there were 64 rural school teachers in Wilkin County for Clarence and Linna to oversee (Gulliford, 1984). In addition, the County Superintendent was often designated as the person who presented the diploma at eighth grade graduation.

It was a big day when the Superintendent arrived for a visit, and in Tenney it was no different. My mother and others clearly remember Linna's visits to the Tenney School as big events when someone quite special was in town. Gertie Kapitan's granddaughter, Barbara Kapitan Holtan, grew up in Nashua and can also remember Linna Gordhamer as being very *important*. Children were told ahead of time of these visits, and were expected to be on their best behavior. Owen Polifka, who attended the Tenney School several years later, remembers that Linna was quite a large woman, but that the students knew in no uncertain terms that there would be no snickering when Mrs. Gordhamer came around. The superintendent sometimes visited the schools unannounced, and sat at the back of the schoolroom to observe the class. These visits could be a source of stress for teachers, as they served as a means through which school inspections were conducted. Teachers were appropriately reprimanded if it was found that the children of Wilkin County were not being properly educated in the manner deemed appropriate by the superintendent. But for the most part, though Linna was "all business," she was a kind person who served as a mentor, teacher, and confidante to many young female school teachers.

Having taught there herself in earlier years, and being familiar with these school children whose families she had known since childhood, I have to believe that the Tenney School was well-represented in Linna's school visit log. She and Clarence lived in Breckenridge during their adult working lives, but Sunday afternoon visits home to Tenney to visit Linna's brothers Fred and Frank and other siblings in the area were well-documented in the "Tenney locals," a newspaper phenomenon which is discussed more in depth later on in Chapter Four. Linna's name frequently appeared in these newspaper accounts, either in her official capacity as Deputy or County Superintendent, or as a Sunday dinner visitor to family members who lived in Tenney in 1928.

While in Breckenridge, Linna was very active in civic life, and seemed to be drawn to service to organizations that were health-oriented and child-oriented. She served on the Wilkin County Nursing Committee starting in 1943; she was chair of the Red Cross Service Committee; she organized polio drives; she volunteered for the Salvation Army, Easter Seals, Cancer Society, and the Association for Retarded Children; and in her positions in education, was actively involved in the Wilkin County Fair school exhibits. She served on the boards of many service organizations. Without children, Linna focused her energy on the school children and the less fortunate of Wilkin County. She was known as an intelligent, somewhat stern, but very fair and kind woman who always had the best interests of children at heart.

Muriel Lee Edner remembers very well a moment at the Memorial Day parade in Campbell, not long after Muriel had attained her teaching credentials, when Linna approached her and asked her if she would be interested in teaching in one of the rural Tenney schools. Muriel indicated to Linna that she was interested, but that her credentials were still at the College and were therefore unavailable for Linna to view. Linna told Muriel Lee not to worry—she knew Muriel Lee's family and it was a good one. So Muriel Lee was hired on the spot and sure enough, she was teaching the next fall at the District 8 School in Wilkin County.

Linna retired from the county superintendency in December, 1966, making it a period of 39 years in which either Clarence or Linna Gordhamer held this position. The gentleman who succeeded Linna in the position was appointed to serve as superintendent for both Ottertail and Wilkin Counties, a sign that rural schools were rapidly diminishing in number. In fact, the County Superintendent position was abolished only four years later, in 1970, when all rural school districts in Minnesota had merged with independent school districts.

The Tenney School had ceased its operation in 1956, after which all its children were sent to neighboring Campbell.

After her retirement, Linna lived in California for a period of time, but ultimately moved back to Minnesota, where she died in 1993, a month before her 93rd birthday. She and Clarence are buried in the Campbell Cemetery. I visited them there. How I wish I could have sat down and chatted with Linna about her years mentoring the young teachers of Wilkin County. I imagine the thousands of lives that were touched by this woman whose roots were firmly planted in the tiny village of Tenney.

CHAPTER 3

- The Storekeepers & Businesswomen -

Nellie

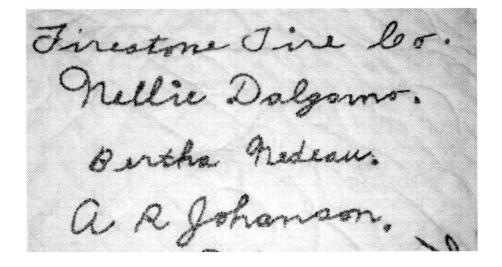

In 1928 Nellie Ida Dalgarno, 32 years old and single, was working as a store clerk in the Klugman Store in Tenney. She was a local farm girl, boarding with my grandfather, A.N. Larson, and family, in the living quarters located on the second floor of Grandpa's General Store. Nellie would have stayed in "Ted's Room," the front bedroom named for my mother's often-visiting Uncle Ted Larson. Nellie had been born in 1896 in the State of Oregon to Nathaniel Dalgarno, a Scottish immigrant, and his wife Joanna "Hannah," a Swedish immigrant. The young family which, at the time included only one-year-old Nellie, moved from Oregon in 1897 to a farm just south of Tenney. Three additional siblings were born after the family arrived in Minnesota.

So, to report for duty at the Klugman Store, Nellie had only to make her way down the outside stairway alongside the Larson Store, walk about thirty feet south on the sidewalk, and into the Klugman Store. Ray Brown of Nashua tells, in the Wilkin County History Book, of a rat contest held in Tenney which involves Nellie, in her position as Klugman Store clerk. This would have been in the time period surrounding the Tenney Quilt. Teams were chosen among a group of young men, and the object of the contest was to be the team that brought in the most rat tails. The winning team was to be served a barbecue supper from the losing team.

Nellie Dalgarno, Klugman Store clerk, was designated as the official counter of rat tails in this competition. Nellie, it seems, had a slight phobia about touching rats. (Who wouldn't, I ask?) So imagine, if you will, boys walking into the Klugman Store, pulling out rat parts from their pockets and depositing them on the store counter in front of Nellie so that their team could be appropriately credited. In an effort to avoid bodily contact with the rat tails, Nellie used a stick to push them across the counter from one spot to another in order to make the official count. When the contestants saw that Nellie was using a stick rather than her hands, the light bulbs in their adolescent brains clicked to bright. Knowing that squeamish Nellie would not touch the merchandise, the boys began to bring in any vegetable root that resembled a rat tail. A meticulously cleaned turnip tail and a little imagination provided a particularly effective interpretation of a rat tail, as long as one did not touch it. Once Nellie caught on to the vegetable caper, she brought the contest to a screeching halt. No winner—no barbecue dinner.

Tenney rat tail lore continues with another incident that surfaced during a chat with one of Gertie Kapitan's grandchildren. It seems as though there may have been another rat tail contest, or perhaps it was the same one mentioned above. Apparently, once rat tails were counted, they were deposited in the outhouse back behind the store. One particularly enterprising youth determined that it would be easier to climb down the outhouse hole and collect rat tails to add to his total than to go out and catch more rats, kill them, and whack off the valuable tails. Sure enough, the young chap did just that. With a little—er—cleaning and polishing, the rat tails were as good as new, and added to his team's count! I don't know who won that contest, but if I were the judge I'd be inclined to spot a few extra points to the guy who jumped into the outhouse hole.

For an extended period of time during the year of 1928, Nellie had been in Minot, North Dakota, but returned home in August. Chances are she was visiting relatives there, as Minot had apparently been a stopping off point for many Dalgarnos on their way out to Montana to homestead. By December of 1928, Nellie had left Minot and moved on to Minneapolis. It would seem that the year of the Tenney Quilt was a major transition year for Nellie as she had lived in Tenney through that summer, Minot in the fall, and Minneapolis later on in the winter, all in one year.

Nellie had heard, most likely from her aunt, Carrie Dalgarno, who lived in the City, that there were factory jobs available for young

women in Minneapolis. She subsequently moved to Minneapolis and found a room on Fourth Avenue South, only about four blocks from the factory at which she would work. Her job would be to assemble heat regulators at the Minneapolis Heat Regulator Company, which would eventually merge with and become the Honeywell Corporation. In addition to factory jobs, the big city provided employment for young women as store clerks, laundresses, domestics of various sorts, and a variety of factory workers. If a young woman had the desire and

Nellie (middle) with friends Elsie Hamann and Effie (last name unknown).

the means to get to the city and to find a place to live, there were jobs available. Both Nellie and her younger sister Isabelle went to work at Honeywell but, while sister Isabelle took to the big city, Nellie apparently felt the call of the prairie, as she returned to Tenney within about a year and a half. Nellie did enjoy occasional trips back to the city for visits and special events, such as in August 1930, when she and her good friend, Lana Hamann hitched a ride to St. Paul with a returning Tenney visitor and took in the Minnesota State Fair. But for the most part, Nellie preferred the less hectic life in Tenney, and had also become more than a little interested in a local bachelor, George Dopp.

Nellie Dalgarno and George Dopp began courting. Perhaps it was a sign of George's efforts to spruce things up a bit for things to come when, in the summer of 1930, "the buildings on the George Dopp farm are enjoying a new coat of paint this week." In June of 1932, Nellie and George were married, and Nellie moved in with George on the farm. There seems to be a bit of a discrepancy in records related to George Dopp's age. If you believe what he reported on his World War I draft registration card, he would have been 42 at the time of his marriage to Nellie. If you believe the 1930 census, he would have been 38. Both being married "later in life," George and Nellie did not have children.

George was born in Iowa but moved with his family to Tenney at some point before 1917. George's connection to Tenney may have been his sister, Edna, who married Arthur Kath, a member of one of Tenney and Campbell's largest families. There are 27 separate Kath relatives listed on the Tenney Quilt, and though I have done some limited research into this large family, I am not sure that I have the fortitude to sort them all out. I do know that William Kath was the patriarch of this family, having fathered 12 children, many of whom stayed in the area and had large families themselves. The Kath family—and remember, in Tenney it was pronounced "Kates"—deserve an entire book of their own.

At any rate, while Nellie was living in Minneapolis, George had been back in Tenney, living in what Gertie Kapitan referred to as his "bachelor apartment" in town. He apparently had both an apartment in town and a farm which I believe had been—or still was—the home of his mother. George took part in the seemingly regular young people card-playing gatherings, even though he would have been quite a bit older than most of the people in that crowd. He was the manager of the Tenney Shipping Association, and in this capacity, often accompanied shipments of cattle to St. Paul. This job was sometimes delegated to other men in town; mentioned at various points in 1928 were Carl

Wahl, Otto Hamann, Louie Wittman, and Walter Kath. In early 1929, the results of the 1928 annual meeting were unofficially reported by the local correspondent, indicating that nearly $50,000 worth of hogs and cattle were shipped during that year. George was a good friend of the Polifkas, my grandmother's family, particularly my grandmother's brother, Cliff, who ran the local tavern, as well as a good friend of my grandfather, A.N. Larson.

Shipping cattle to the St. Paul Stockyards was a regular occurrence in Tenney in 1928. Railroads had reached Tenney in 1885—43 years earlier—and Tenney's very existence is owed to the arrival of the railroad. The railroad route determined the location of most villages in the area, as towns built up where a rail siding (a short-distance, parallel set of tracks) had been constructed. In fact Tenney was named for John P. Tenney, a Minneapolis lumberman who gave land in order for the Soo Line Railroad to go through. Tenney's son-in-law, Fred Maechler, owned the quarter section of land north of the tracks which became the town site, and he built the first home in town. The village of Tenney was incorporated in 1902. The Soo Line was the lifeline of Tenney—cattle, hogs, store inventory, mail, grain, and people moved in and out of Tenney on a daily basis. Virtually every person's life was changed by the arrival and subsequent development of the railroad. A trip to the Twin Cities—or anywhere more than ten or twenty miles—was most likely taken by train if the railroad served such a place, and it was a common sight to see someone greeting a friend or relative on the platform as the traveler stepped off the train at the Tenney depot. Evadna Waite was usually given the task of greeting her grandmother, Mrs. Wilson, at the train depot when she came to Tenney to visit her family. As a young teenager in the Twenties, Evadna was embarrassed to stand at the platform and greet Grandma, who always stepped off the train with a dish towel on her head. I suppose it's sort of like going to pick up your teenager at school in curlers and a bathrobe, with Barry Manilow music blasting from the car radio and the windows wide open.

Grandma Wilson was the same person who attended the Tenney Sunday School picnic, held in a park at Wahpeton wearing a beautiful new—formal—blue full-length dress, thinking it was perfectly appropriate for such an event. The skirt swirled as she walked, creating what Grandma apparently felt was a beautiful and elegant impression. Clearly she felt good wearing it. Her daughter, Grace Waite, had tried to convince Grandma Wilson to wear something a bit more casual, but Grandma insisted on looking her best. Part of the festivity of the picnic was a small traveling zoo for the pleasure of the Sunday School kids. The long, swirling bright blue skirt was just too tempting for a sweet little monkey which was part of this exhibition, so the little guy grabbed Grandma Wilson's skirt as she walked by and hung on—with the grip of a gorilla. One can only imagine the fracas as Grandma Wilson stubbornly and with a great amount of grunting, groaning and sweating, laid claim to her skirt, trying to muscle it away from the monkey's grip, calling the critter every name in her extensive vocabulary. The monkey, equally as determined, hung onto the other end, probably in a heightened state of terror. In the end, the monkey successfully retained a large chunk of Grandma Wilson's beautiful blue dress and I imagine it took Grandma Wilson some time to recover from that incident.

One person often mentioned in conjunction with the railroad was Sam Iler who, in census records, was generally identified as a "laborer." In the late Twenties, he often helped unload loads of coal for the Farmers' Elevator, and was called upon often to help load or unload other railroad freight. Sam also helped load up shipments of stock on their way to the St. Paul Stockyards. Sam had a reputation for being—well—an ornery fella. And perhaps he had every right to be, based on "the wash water incident" that occurred much later. One fine winter day during the holiday season, Sam was walking north on the sidewalk on Main Street in Tenney, headed toward the Post Office to mail a handful of Christmas cards, no doubt prepared by his wife, Ruby. He was in front of Cliff's Place, the local tavern. Grace Polifka, from the outside step of her second-floor home over Cliff's Place, just happened to throw a pail of wash water down at precisely the moment that Sam was passing by below. Sam Iler may have been in the right place, but was unfortunately there at the wrong time. He was fully doused with dirty wash water. Reactions by various townspeople who may have witnessed this scene probably varied from sheer terror to

unabashed amusement, but Sam clearly saw no humor in the situation. He was sufficiently disgusted with Grace that he did not speak to
her for at least a year afterwards.

George Dopp, as a frequent traveler by train to the stockyards,
was most likely the connection to three families whose names appear
on the Tenney Quilt. They are seemingly connected to Tenney only by
their association with the St. Paul Stockyards. These signers are (a)
Dinty Boyce and his wife, Elsie, who lived in St. Paul, where Dinty
was in livestock sales at the stockyards; (b) Norris K. (N.K.) Carnes,
his wife Elizabeth, and their children, also named N.K. and Elizabeth.
N.K., Sr. was the assistant manager of a livestock association and lived
in St. Paul; and (c) W.G. Metcalf, also of St. Paul, whose occupation
was listed as "Livestock commission."

George and Nellie Dopp remained active in the social life of
Tenney after their marriage. George was a fun-loving, social guy with
a wide circle of friends, who was prone to playing practical jokes at
times. He was a frequent hunting partner of my great grandfather,
John Polifka. He once invited several friends to enjoy a sumptuous
feast of venison roast, only to report to them after dinner that he had
actually served them a "poor little lamb," which caused temporary
upset for a few of the women in attendance.

Meanwhile, George's slightly more proper Nellie belonged to the
Ladies Aid, as well as Tenney's Bridge Club. Mrs. Parks and Helen
Polifka also played bridge with the group, as well as Helen's daughters Audrey and Myrtle, daughter-in-law Grace Polifka, Vesta Gore,
and Ethel Kugler. Card playing was clearly a very popular activity
in Tenney among both the men and the women, somewhat surprising
to me given the aversion among some immigrants of that generation
to card playing due to its association with gambling. *Bridge*, *Rook*,
500, and *Bunco* seem to be the most mentioned card games played
in the Tenney social circles in the Twenties, really not much different
than the traditional card games played today. Nellie preferred these
more traditional activities, and also took part in a type of entertainment that I believe only Minnesotans find entertaining—that is, looking at the crops. The Tenney locals document Nellie taking a "joy
ride" with her friend, Mary Hamann, to view the crops on a Sunday

afternoon in late August.

George and Nellie remained in the Tenney area the rest of their lives, settling eventually in Wheaton. It seems that most people who left Tenney later in life retired to one of three places: Wheaton, Fairmount (North Dakota), or Breckenridge. George and Nellie lived long lives. George died in 1975, at age 85, and Nellie died nine years later at age 88. Nellie had fallen and suffered a broken hip and was living in a nursing home at the time of her death from heart attack.

Nellie made a few forays into the world as a young woman, perhaps seeking to find a world beyond what she had always known. But she always returned to the comfort and familiarity of Tenney and its surroundings, the land her father and mother had come from afar to homestead when Nellie was just a year old.

Audrey

In 1928, Audrey Jeannette Polifka was 24 years old and living at home with her parents in Tenney. Born in 1904, she was the third of five children of John and Helen Polifka. Audrey was to be my grandmother. I always knew Grandma as quite a reserved person so I have assumed she always had that demeanor, even as a young person, and I think I am correct for the most part. Whereas Audrey's social activities as a young 24-year-old woman in 1928 are documented now and then in the Tenney news column, they do not rival those of her older sister, LaVanche, whose story is told later in this chapter. However, I would be remiss in saying that Audrey didn't kick her heels up now and then.

It wasn't until I looked through some of my grandmother's old photo albums that I found a different side of my grandmother—a playful, fun-loving side that I hadn't seen before and which was a joy to see. As far as I had previously known and heard, Audrey had pretty much done all the normal, unremarkable things—go to school, graduate, take part in church activities, learn all the homemaking and handwork skills, and occasionally run off to a moving picture with her friends. What a wonderful surprise to find some small, soft-leather, black-paged photo albums chock full of photos of Audrey as a 20 to 25-year-old and her friends. There were road trips to various points in South Dakota—Sisseton, Brandon, Aberdeen—with pictures of Audrey and her four female traveling partners, all in their one-piece cotton dresses and heels. They are standing by fences, standing by bridges, sitting in the grass, two friends together, then another combination of two, then four, then the whole group standing by the car. The common denominator is a smile on every face, arms around shoulders, and a sense of freedom and joy that only a road trip can provide a bunch of 20-something young ladies. And then there are the photos of Audrey and her friends dressed up for any one of several of Tenney's masquerade balls, holiday parties, and other special events. One has Audrey and friend Clara dressed as a Dutch couple, complete with wooden shoes—man and woman, with Audrey as the man—hugging each other and laughing. Another shows a smiling Audrey and sister LaVanche in matching pirate outfits. One of my favorites has four bums lined up on the road—the bums are Audrey, Ann Janke, Jennie Richardson, and an unidentified girl, each with baggy men's clothes, yukking it up and clearly quite proud of their get-up. There are photos of Audrey and her good friend, Laura Scott, and others with friends Daisy Pithey, Elsie Hamann, and lots with sister Myrtle—just being goofy. And there are friends "Fritz," "Buzz," and "Lundy." Audrey enjoyed life as a young Tenney woman and had many friends. As it turns out, she didn't sit at home all day making doilies.

From these same photographs, clearly Audrey enjoyed the company of a blonde-haired young man named Ivan Smith, a very handsome, muscular specimen featured in several photos, sometimes standing with Audrey, sometimes with arms happily but somewhat tentatively around each others' shoulders. If Audrey wasn't Ivan's sweetheart, I'm certain she wished she was. At any rate, in spite of the above, Audrey would still have been considered relatively reserved compared to her older sister LaVanche and younger sister Myrtle, and was probably more comfortable emulating the "follower" role of her mother, Helen Polifka.

Jean Schwinn, in her Waite family history tells of the courtship of Grace Waite (Schwinn, 1984), whose name appears on the quilt. Audrey and Grace were friends later in life, as Grace was about 15 years older than Audrey. When Grace's future husband, Earl, was attending school at "the Little Red School" in rural Tenney, he appar-

Audrey (second from right) and pals.

ently was significantly irritated by Grace, and was prone to repeatedly say mean things about "that Grace Wilson." Earl would leave the house when Grace came to visit his sisters. Earl decided to express his disgust for this annoying classmate by naming one of his two ugly horses after her. A girl named Minnie apparently elicited the same reaction from him, as the ugly equines were "Grace" and "Minnie." Grace then moved away from Tenney with her family, but she reappeared in Tenney as a schoolteacher years later. They started dating! Earl and Grace were married in 1910. I sincerely hope the horse was dead by then.

Audrey graduated from the eighth grade at the Tenney School

and like many other Tenney kids, went on to Campbell High School. She and her sister Myrtle were the only high school graduates in the family. Audrey's father had the rural mail route in Tenney and when he had to be gone, such as when he and Helen would attend an out-of-town funeral, Audrey sometimes took care of the mail, as did her brother Cliff. The Polifkas pretty much kept the rural mail route in the family in those days. Other than her back-up postal duties, I know of no other employment in Audrey's late teens and early 20s. Maybe she was just having too much fun.

The Polifka family lived directly behind the Larson Store in Tenney and of course in a town of that size, they knew the A.N. Larson family well. A.N. Larson, my grandfather, was born in 1885 in Stockholm, Minnesota, and was first married to Linda Hertrich, with whom he had two sons, Ralph and Andrew. A.N. had come to Tenney in 1912 to purchase the general merchandise store from Mr. Simonitch who, along with a Mr. Hanson, had built the store and operated it for several years prior to my grandfather's arrival. For A.N., purchasing the store was a culminating event in a series of store clerk jobs in other towns to prepare him for business ownership. He had previously been employed in a grocery and dry goods store in Vernon, South Dakota, and a department store in Cooperstown, North Dakota. A.N. had met Linda, a nurse, after arriving in Tenney, when he was hospitalized in Breckenridge. Linda was a popular, active person in the Tenney women's network, and once married to A.N., she worked as a sales clerk in the family store. Their young family lived on the second floor. Each February, A.N. and Linda took the train to Minneapolis to do their buying for the upcoming year. Leisure pursuits were not easy to fit in, but A.N. enjoyed hunting and fishing with his sons, activities that were usually limited to Sunday afternoons due to the commitments of small town store ownership.

The years immediately surrounding the quilt, 1928 to 1931, were significant—and tragic—for the Larson family. Linda developed Tuberculosis and over the course of the year of 1928, her health declined to the point that she became bedridden. During the summer and fall of 1928, precisely the time that signatures were being gathered for the Tenney Quilt, Linda was seen by doctors several times, and finally had an extended stay at Mayo Clinic in Rochester that fall and had surgery. She passed away in January, 1929 at the age of 42, leaving behind a husband and two teenage sons. This was a big deal in Tenney, losing an upstanding citizen such as Linda, and at a young age to boot. Local Tenney girl, Audrey Polifka, had presumably begun to work at the Larson Store around the time Linda became ill, filling in when Linda was no longer able to help.

About a year after Linda's death, it became apparent to A.N. and Audrey that they had more than just a working relationship. Tenney news articles gave some clues into their brief courtship, with reports of ice skating outings to Campbell during the winter months of early 1930 with A.N., Audrey and the boys, as well as Sunday afternoon excursions together to Ten Mile Lake that summer of 1930. Despite a 19-year age difference, A.N. and Audrey were married in September,

My grandmother, Audrey Polifka.

1930. A.N. celebrated his upcoming marriage with the purchase of a brand new 1930 Chevrolet late that summer.

I have often wondered about the relationship of my grandfather, A.N., and grandmother, Audrey. Though they certainly must have loved each other, they weren't the sort to outwardly show affection for each other. Once I heard the story of their lives, I somehow developed the perception that Audrey's initial attraction to A.N. was more a matter of compassionately stepping in to take care of A.N. after the loss of his young wife than of falling madly in love with the man of her dreams. And from A.N.'s perspective, here was a hardworking, kind, reserved young woman who worked for him and knew his store, provided a woman's touch in his family of men, and came from a respectable family that A.N. had known since he first arrived in Tenney. I will never know if my perception of their "marriage of convenience" was correct or not and perhaps I should not know, as those sorts of things are best left in the hearts of those who lived them. What I do know is that they, together, were my grandparents, who took good care of their daughter—my mother—and whose home was always a place of love and warmth to me as a child.

After their marriage in Tenney, Audrey moved in with A.N. and the boys to the Larson home above the store. The living quarters contained a kitchen along the back of the house. Off the north side of the kitchen was a pantry which, in the winter, housed a chemical toilet. Lovely! Off the opposite side of the kitchen was a covered sleeping porch, initially built so that A.N.'s first wife, Linda, who had Tuberculosis, could sleep more comfortably and breathe fresh air. After Linda's death, this covered porch served as the laundry and bathing area, with a ringer washer and a large round wash tub for my mother's Saturday night bath. The wash water for laundry and Saturday night baths came from the rain barrel at the top of the back stairs. The home had a large central dining room which housed the heating stove, the radio, and the dining table. The dining room table later served as the meeting place for the Tenney School Board, on which Audrey served, along with Jack Richardson and Jim Janke. The dining room greeted family and guests as they entered the home from the front stairs, which ran alongside the outside of the building, with the bottom step on Main Street. A smaller living room area was at the front of the home, with two windows facing out on to Tenney's main street. There were three bedrooms—A.N. and Audrey's nearer the back, my mother's in the middle, and a guest bedroom room in the front which was always known as "Ted's Room." When it was time for dinner, Audrey banged on the stove pipe, which A.N. then heard from his store below and walked upstairs.

Behind the Larson Store were two buildings: the outhouse, and a building called "the shed," which was efficiently used for four different purposes: one room to store coal, one room full of vinegar barrels and other warehoused goods, one room—a chicken coop in a previous life—used as my mother's playhouse, and finally, a snug little single car garage.

At the time A.N. and Audrey were married, the boys were attending high school in Elbow Lake, Minnesota, so were home only on the weekends and during the summer. Tragically, son Andrew was killed in a hunting accident only one year later, at age 17. He had begun his college career at the North Dakota State School of Science in Wahpeton only one month earlier. So in the course of two and a half years, A.N. lost his young wife, remarried, and lost his eldest son. He was lucky to have Audrey to help him pick up the pieces and support him during what must have been an awful time.

The circumstances of Andrew's death were indeed tragic. It was in the fall, with pheasant hunting on the minds of the Larson boys, 17-year-old Andrew and 16-year-old Ralph. They were with their friends, Orval Wittman and Paul Roser, the minister's son, and were traveling by automobile to a hunting destination south of Wheaton. Ralph and Andrew were in the front seat, with Ralph driving, and Orval and Paul were in the back. At some point in the journey, the boys spotted some pheasants by the side of the road and in their excitement, hurriedly pulled over and prepared to get out of the car to take a shot or two. In the commotion of the moment, Paul Roser's loaded gun accidentally discharged from the back seat, firing through the passenger-side car seat and hitting Andrew in the back, just above the hip. This happened at about 3:00 in the afternoon, and Andrew died that evening around 11:00 p.m. During the time between the accident and his death, Andrew was awake and aware of what was going on. He voiced his disappointment that, because of his injury, he would be unable to play basketball that winter for the college basketball team. Andrew, long and lean, was a gifted athlete, playing the starting Center position on his high school basketball team, and had hoped to continue his basketball career in college.

The beauty of this story lies in what happened after Andrew died. My grandfather, A.N. Larson, had to have felt like a beaten man. He had lost his wife only two years prior, and now his first-born son. A.N. went to Paul Roser, the young man whose gun had killed Andrew, put his arm around Paul's shoulder, and told him that there was no reason for two families to suffer. This was an accident, and he—Paul—was forgiven. A.N. was a compassionate man and a man of principle, and I am very proud of him when I think of that act of kindness. The two men remained friends throughout the rest of their lives, and Paul Roser served as a pall bearer at Grandpa A.N.'s funeral many years later.

The year of the Tenney Quilt, 1928, the Larson Store served as the center of action in Tenney. By this time, A.N. Larson, my grandfather, had been running the store for sixteen years and was a well-established and well-respected businessman. Most people in town entered its doors frequently. When not engaged with his customers, A.N. did his bookwork while sitting at his roll-top desk in the store. The roll top was always rolled up—ready for action. Occasionally A.N. sat at his desk and perused *The Saturday Evening Post*, a magazine that was accessed regularly, for years, at the Larson home.

In the words of the booklet printed for Tenney's centennial celebration, "A.N. Larson's store had <u>everything</u> anyone would ever need!" The Larson Store carried dry goods such as shoes and boots, hats, work gloves, and probably silk stockings. One could buy Scott Tissue, Bulova watches, paper products, and Lysol Disinfectant. After 1928, when the Janke Hardware closed, A.N. carried more items such as crushed oyster shells [for chickens], salt blocks for livestock use, cleaning supplies, and other non-food provisions.

The store carried towels, shelf cloth, handkerchiefs, and fabric. Chances are that the Larson Store's fabric selection did not rival the selection of the J.C. Penney store in the larger neighboring town of Breckenridge. A 1928 J.C. Penney advertisement in the *Breckenridge Gazette* advertised pillow tubing and shirting fabric for 29¢ per yard, "dainty check patterns for fresh undies" at 39¢ per yard, as well as rayon "to make charming undies." Based on this marketing approach, apparently it was quite desirable to have undies that were both "fresh" and "charming." A.N. Larson probably did not bother with undies fabric but more likely carried the more practical poplin and shirtings by the yard, as well as thread, patterns, embroidery floss, thimbles, and needles.

But the Larson Store's principal business was in the food items. Town customers shopped during the week, when A.N. was open until 6:00 p.m. every evening, six days a week, plus Wednesday and Saturday nights. Farmers and neighboring country folks often came in during those evening hours. Very often this jaunt to town was a family event that warranted a bath, clean clothes, and a hat. The woman of the house was generally in charge of purchasing the groceries and other weekly provisions, while the men gathered at Cliff's Place for card playing, pool, a cigarette, and perhaps a glass or two of beer. The women gave A.N. their list of needed items and in the winter sat around the old coal stove and visited as A.N. filled their orders. During daytime visits to town during the week, farmers brought in cream, which A.N. then packaged and sent on to the creamery in Fairmount, North Dakota, the next town west on the Soo Line.

Bananas initially came in on the whole stalk, and Grandpa had devised a hook and pulley system used to get the bananas down for customers. There was a large flat display table about a yard square, with oranges perched precariously in a pyramid pattern. Cookies came in cardboard boxes which fit into a glass-front metal frame for easy access. Brown sugar and vinegar were in crocks under the counter. *Home Brand* canned goods lined the shelves on one side of the store from floor to ceiling, with a "can grabber" hanging nearby to fetch items on the top shelves. Swift's Silverleaf brand pure lard could be purchased by the box or in two-, four- or eight-pound pails. A candy case held such goodies as cream-filled chocolate mounds and a variety of hard candies. Bubble gum had recently come onto the scene in 1928. Customers could find Williams Mug Shaving soap, Pebeco toothpaste, Woodbury's Facial Soap, Listerine mouthwash, Unguentine ointment, Ponds Cold Cream and Lux detergent. A glass cabinet held snuff and chewing tobacco. If you needed a pack of Lucky Strikes, a trip next door to the tavern would be necessary. Gereta Kath, wife of Clarence, in her demureness, was a bit embarrassed to request toilet paper out loud, so whispered in A.N.'s ear the need to add this to her list, and he discreetly obliged. Peter Pan peanut butter, though a bit pricey, was beginning to be quite a popular food that could be stretched to feed large numbers of children or hired hands.

The mystery as to why the *Kellogg's Cereal Company* name would appear on the Tenney Quilt was solved in a discussion with

Barbara Holtan, the granddaughter of Matt and Gertie Kapitan and daughter of E.W. (Everett) Kapitan, whose name appears on the quilt. In the same square as Matt and Gertie are the names of Mae Engfer and her husband, George. Mae was Gertie Kapitan's sister. The **Kellogg's Cereal Company** name appears directly above George Engfer. Barbara recalled a photograph of her Uncle George Engfer standing in front of a big Kellogg's panel truck. So apparently George gave a 10-cent donation in the name of his employer, Kellogg's Cereal Company, which is now forever connected to the Tenney Quilt. It is probably quite appropriate that Kellogg's is included, as the Larson Store no doubt sold the popular Kellogg's breakfast foods. Research of the Kellogg Cereal Company revealed that 1928 was the year in which Kellogg introduced Rice Krispies to the market. Prior to this, Kellogg's had only two other breakfast cereals, Corn Flakes and All Bran (Kellogg NA Co, 2007).

A big roll of brown paper was bolted to one end of the sales counter, and a ball of string hung in a little metal string cage from the ceiling. Dry goods and bulk food items often went home wrapped in brown paper with a string around it, with canned goods and other grocery items sometimes traveling home in a cardboard box or basket. Kerosene and vinegar usually went home in containers brought in with the customer. Paper bags, not used in 1928, would come later.

Most of the store's stock came to Tenney by Soo Line Railroad. When the school bell rang at the end of the day, several of the young boys raced the one-block distance from the school yard to the railroad depot to check if there were packages labeled for the Larson Store. They knew that Mr. Larson would pay them a nickel for as much as they could carry from the depot to the store. This provided a service to the store, as well as some discretionary spending money for the boys—money that probably went right back into the store coffers in exchange for cookies, candy, or other things important to the knicker-clad boys of Tenney in 1928.

As purveyors of items ranging from kerosene to liniment to work boots to canned peaches, A.N. and Audrey became, de facto, the town's consultants in shoe repair, home remedies, nutrition, sewing, and who knows what else. The store provided Audrey with customer service experience that would serve her well in her later career at the drugstore in Glenwood.

Tenney's Town Hall, used for most of the social events in town, had a large stage curtain with a pastoral scene of hills and a valley in the middle, and advertising around the edges. One of those advertisements was for the A.N. Larson Store that read "A.N. Larson & Co. General Merchandise, Staples & Various Sundries." The curtain's color scheme was primarily shades of brown and gold. The stage was later taken out of the town hall in the 1940s so that the building could be used as a roller rink. My mother has often said she wished she could have salvaged that curtain when it was removed, in order to preserve the Larson Store advertisement. But like so many things, the curtain only seemed valuable once she looked back through the lens of a lifetime of experiences and realized its significance.

The chain store concept seemed to take hold in the Twenties, with A&P being a prime example. The A&P stores were relatively small, and offered no major frills, but their low prices during these lean times resulted in the 15,000 stores nationwide by 1930 (Gwynn, 2007) . These chain stores were reserved, of course, for the larger cities, but were definitely a presence in Wilkin County. Lloyd Dawson, who spent some time playing cards at Tenney's pool hall, apparently talked about how he could buy cigarette tobacco at the new A&P in Breckenridge for two cents cheaper per tin that he could buy it in Tenney. The Larson General Store still provided most of the daily needs for the citizens of Tenney in the Twenties, Thirties and Forties, but Grandpa no doubt felt increasing pressure as people became more mobile and thus more comfortable and able to do their shopping in the larger towns in the area—Wahpeton and Breckenridge, known as "the little twins," and Wheaton.

Two years after A.N. and Audrey's marriage, in 1932, a daughter, Helen Johanna, was born. Her arrival must have been particularly pleasing to A.N., whose previous children had been only boys, one of whom had been tragically killed just one year prior. Helen Johanna was named after her two grandmothers, but was called "Helen Jo," "Jo," or "Joey" by her parents and Tenney folks in general. Helen Jo was to become my mother. With her half-brother Andrew having died before she was born, and half-brother Ralph away at high school and then immediately off to college, Helen Jo grew up as an only child, living a relatively happy and comfortable childhood as the daughter of a successful storekeeper and civic leader. Helen Jo attended high school in Campbell like most other Tenney kids, but after one year there, was convinced by her friend, Ruth Ann Ahlstein, to accompany her to what was then known as the Morris Ag School. Helen Jo's late teenage years, after graduating from the Morris Ag School, coincided with her parents' decision to sell the store and move from Tenney in 1947. By this time, Tenney had become in 15-year-old Helen Jo's eyes a somewhat depressing place, with perhaps 30 or 35 people—if you included the family pets—and she was more than willing to pull up roots and head out of town. I suppose Audrey had some of the same feelings but at the same time, Tenney was the only home she had ever known, other than a three-year homesteading stint in South Dakota which is presented later in this chapter. Audrey had been born in Tenney 43 years earlier, and her aging mother still lived in the home in which Audrey was born. It certainly must have been with mixed feelings that Audrey moved away from Tenney.

A.N.'s decision to sell the store was probably met with a sense of relief and satisfaction, but also of sadness. Tenney had provided A.N. with a good living, a place where his three children had been raised, a host of lifelong friends, and a place where he had lost his wife, Linda, and son, Andrew. He sold his business, but kept a cigar box chock full of uncollected debts from customers who bought on credit. But the box remained full. A.N. would not have dreamed of asking his friends to pony up if they were financially not able to do so. He sold the store and its inventory to Leonard and Opal Hardie, who continued to operate the store as a General Mercantile. Within a short period of time, the Hardies moved themselves and the store's contents next door into the old Klugman Store, which remains standing today, though in a dilapidated state. The Klugman building had been converted to a residence and eventually served as the summer home for Opal Hardie and her second husband, Dave Roach, who spent the winter enjoying the warmer climate of Texas. The original Larson Store building was demolished, leaving an empty lot that was never filled with anything except a new crop of grass each spring.

My mother, after she had moved from Tenney, was told by her parents that the store had been moved to Wheaton, apparently to spare her the sadness she may have felt if she had known that her childhood home had been bulldozed. For her entire adulthood until 2007, Helen Jo believed that the building had been moved to Wheaton. The true answer came from Al Manthie, a long-time Tenney resident who served as village clerk for 40 years and was, for all practical purposes, the town's loving and dedicated caretaker for many decades. One day in the 1980s, Al drove up and down the few streets in Tenney and spoke into a tape recorder about the history of every lot and every building. I read the script of this tour, which revealed the fact that the Larson Store building had, in fact, been demolished, not moved to Wheaton. Al's account at that time would be a very reliable source of information.

I had made a few personal pilgrimages to Wheaton in 2006 in 2007 to try to find the Larson Store building before learning that it was never moved. At the time, I realized that it would have been a miracle to actually find it, given the time that had elapsed and the potential for the building to be gone by then, or perhaps more likely, updated or dilapidated to the point of being unrecognizable. I was searching for that sense of familiarity and connectedness—the same that I had sought as I stood on that broken-up, overgrown sidewalk in Tenney. I did enjoy pondering the "next life" of my grandfather's store, and it was a source of mystery and intrigue for me for a period of time. One particular search in Wheaton for the Larson Building occurred in the summer of 2007 with my mother and father. The three of us spent quite a bit of time cruising the streets of Wheaton in what would obviously be a vain attempt at locating the building. The joy was in the search, however, as we, in our quest for "old timers," struck up conversations with several folks in town who, as it turned out, all had connections of some sort with Tenney. One of them, Vern Janke, spent his early childhood in Tenney, and with a smile on his face, remembered stealing candy from the A.N. Larson Store as a young child. Another, Lynn Propp, had grown up in rural Tenney, and had moved Doc Doleman's house from Tintah to Wheaton later in his life. Doc Doleman was related to our family through marriage, and my mother had been in the house as a young child. I knocked, unknowingly, on the door of that house that day in Wheaton, and had a delightful chat with Mr. Propp.

From Tenney, A.N. and Audrey moved to Glenwood, Minnesota, where Audrey's sister LaVanche was living. They bought a home that I would know, through my childhood, as "Grandpa and Grandma's house." My mother lived in this home only as a transition between young adult pursuits such as jobs and an education in the Twin Cities, and was soon swept away by a handsome young man visiting a friend in Glenwood, a man that would become my father, Earl Leaf.

Though A.N. had retired when he moved to Glenwood, Audrey was still of working age, so she secured a job at the local drug store. As it turned out, Audrey would spend over 30 years in that store. She worked as a store clerk and also did the welfare billing for many years. I can remember so many trips to that drugstore as a child—even as a young adult—walking in the door as our family had just arrived in town for a visit, and seeing Grandma there waiting on a customer, looking up with a big smile once she heard "Hi Grandma!" And Grandma, in her role as store clerk at Corner Drug, was for many years my personal Christmas gift shopper. I would come into the store with a certain amount of money, Grandma would help me choose appropriate gifts (I particularly remember a nutcracker for my dad and some Jean Naté bath powder for my mother), and then Grandma would gift wrap them. She had a particular knack and took great pride in her gift wrapping skills, making sure the wrapping paper was taut and all the corners were squared and taped neatly. I can picture now her hands, gnarled with Rheumatoid Arthritis at a young age, making perfect looking packages with perfect bows. Strangely enough, there always seemed to be enough money in my pocket to cover whatever gift I wanted to buy. Grandma would tell me that almost any item was "on sale." I didn't realize until my early teenage years that the Corner Drug really did not have a lot of sales; rather, my sweet Grandma Aud was supplementing my meager gift budget. I would walk out of the store with meticulously wrapped gifts in hand, ready to proudly place them under the Christmas tree.

A.N. was doing pull-ups on an iron pull-up bar in his basement until well into his seventies. He smoked cigars down in that basement with his brother-in-law, Erick, and had a nifty little porcelain donkey sitting on a basement shelf which dispensed a cigarette out of its mouth when I pulled up on its tail. Or maybe it was the other way around and the cigarette came out the donkey's back end. At any rate, I do remember being slightly amused at its irreverence. I don't remember that Grandpa smiled a lot, but I remember that he was very tender and patient with me, and always happy to see us when we visited. And he always had fudge-striped shortbread cookies and banana flavored circus peanuts in a certain kitchen cupboard. Both treats were kept in glass jars. I could go to that kitchen right now and pick out the exact cupboard door. Perhaps this is what inspired the presence of a "treat bucket" in my home as my own children were growing up—a gallon-sized plastic ice cream bucket filled with goodies—always in the same spot on the same shelf in the pantry. My own little granddaughter, Raea, now has her own "treat bucket" when she comes to visit Nanny and Grandpa. I believe I will soon start stocking it with circus peanuts.

Near the end of his life, Grandpa A.N. was hospitalized for complications from a nerve disorder in his jaw that shot excruciating jabs of pain along his jaw and across his face at frequent intervals. He courageously endured the pain for a period of time, but eventually had to be hospitalized at the Fergus Falls State Hospital so that he could be restrained and prevented from harming himself. The pain had simply become too much to bear. Before his death he was transferred to the hospital in Glenwood, where he died in 1967 at the age of 82, an event that, at age 11, I remember well. I have only, in recent years, come to know the degree of respect that A.N. had garnered throughout his life, particularly in Tenney. No matter who I spoke to, when I brought up the name of A.N. Larson, they would inevitably say such things as "A.N. treated people with kindness and respect, no matter who they were" or "A.N. was one of the finest men I ever knew." I have wondered, sometimes, if this was one of God's purposes for leading me to this project. I have come to know the people who made me who I am. And I have not been disappointed at what I have learned.

After A.N.'s death, Audrey sold the house and moved to an apartment in downtown Glenwood. She worked at Corner Drug until she reached the age of 80. She was known there as a friendly, quiet, polite salesperson, and a hard worker. She was still mentally sharp at the time of her retirement and always dressed very well, never wearing what I would have referred to at the time as "old lady" clothes. Grandma always wore earrings and a necklace—which always matched. She lived independently after her retirement in her apartment. Too claustrophobic to climb into the aging elevator, Audrey hiked up and down the two flights of stairs several times a day despite her painful arthritic knees. She drove a little aqua blue putt-putt Rambler.

When Audrey's daughter Helen Jo and husband—my parents— moved to New London, Minnesota and built a new home, Audrey moved in, and spent her last years in New London. She eventually moved to a local nursing home. She was content at the nursing home, as she roomed with her sister, LaVanche, for several years. My dear Grandma Aud died in 1999, after reaching the age of 95. Throughout her life, even as her body failed and dementia cruelly stole her logical thought processes, I always saw her as a quiet, kind, dignified person. I have nothing but happy memories of this girl turned woman turned grandma, whose life was shaped by the little town of Tenney.

LaVanche

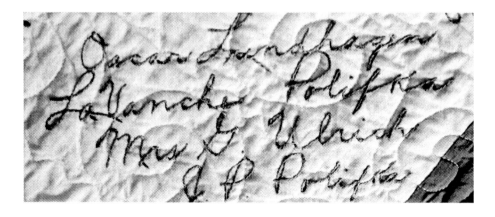

LaVanche was unique. She was a mover and shaker in the village of Tenney—an instigator, a jokester, a persistent, stubborn, active girl.

In 1928, she was 29 years old and had moved from Tenney to Wheaton and was working as a banker. LaVanche was the second child of John Peter and Helen Polifka, my great grandparents, born in 1899. Given that her older brother had died in infancy, LaVanche grew up in the role of oldest child in the family. She grew up in Tenney, and attended the Tenney School. Not completing high school, LaVanche instead went to work in the Tenney Bank, and then through sheer persistence, stubbornness, and ambition, moved on to other professional positions of which most young Tenney girls of that era perhaps would not dare dream.

LaVanche did handwork and baked bread and canned tomatoes and all of those things that young women did or were supposed to do at the turn of the century in rural Minnesota. But she also played cards and went to dances in the Town Hall and wasn't afraid to kick up her heels. She was assertive, confident, and modern, and probably questioned authority more than once. Though still quite conservative herself, LaVanche was a young woman who most likely challenged many of the behavioral guidelines dictated by a small, conservative town. She no doubt expressed her opinion about most things and didn't apologize for it. For instance, LaVanche was not a happy camper when her brother Cliff purchased the fixtures and goods of Frank McGee's tavern in 1927 and declared his intention to operate a tavern in Tenney. When the Tenney Bank closed in the 1928-1929 timeframe—right about the time the quilt was created—Cliff converted the bank building into a pool hall, with living quarters upstairs. LaVanche did not hesitate telling her younger brother how she felt about having a tavern and pool hall in the family, and she forever after referred to Cliff's business as an ice cream parlor—NEVER a "tavern" or "pool hall." After all, you *could* buy ice cream there. One person who was *not* disgusted about this business development was young Muriel Lee Edner who remembers, as a toddler, proudly walking hand-in-hand with her beloved grandpa, John Polifka, to Cliff's Place in anticipation of an ice cream cone, a rare and special treat.

In a mock wedding at the occasion of Hattie Richardson's bridal shower, LaVanche was costumed as the *father* of the bride. I'm sure she was the only girl who volunteered for that position. Photos of

LaVanche and her friend Elsie Hamann, as teenagers, show two happy-go-lucky knicker-clad teenage girls with elbows linked together and sporting proud, happy smiles. At the Royal Neighbors costume ball in 1928, LaVanche came as a pirate and left with the first prize trophy. Seemingly she was one of the primary players in the social network of Tenney in the late 1910s and early 1920s. She lived life with gusto.

LaVanche's father, John Polifka, had come to the Tenney area as a farm laborer at age 26, finding work on the John and Emma Ready farm. The Readys and Polifkas had been acquaintances in Dodge County, Wisconsin prior to coming to Tenney, so the Readys knew John Polifka to be a solid young man who would work hard. John had good reason to retain a harmonious relationship with his boss, and that was their daughter, Helen, who would become his wife just four years later, in 1896. After their marriage, John and Helen farmed for four years, then moved to town when they purchased a small general store in Tenney. Helen ran the store while "J.P.", as he was sometimes called, managed the Osborn-McMillan Elevator. They moved their business across the street to a different building—one that would in later years house Janke Hardware—and it became primarily a grocery store, as well as the town's post office. J.P. was Tenney's first postmaster and later became the rural mail carrier.

Unable to quell the desire to own his own land, John sold the store in 1908 and set out on an adventure that would test him in every way a person could be tested. Land was available in South Dakota, so John, along with his wife Helen and their four children ages nine, six, four, and two, filed a claim in what is now Perkins County, South Dakota. With them were two other families—John's sister Julia and family, which included brother-in-law John Stoffel and three little girls ages six, four and one. Also with the group was friend James Hannon, manager of the Farmers Elevator in Tenney, and his family. They felt that, by supporting each other and with God's help, they could find their way and make it through whatever challenges life would deal them.

The John Polifka family arrived on the barren prairie late in the fall, but time enough to build a 14 x 24 sod house. The structure had a wood roof and floor and was lined with corrugated steel, the entire home heavily fortified with sod from the prairie. The nearest railroad was in Lemmon, South Dakota, nearly 60 miles away, so all provisions including wood, household and farm goods were hauled by horse and wagon. John was able to clear 10 acres of land that fall. Tragedy fell on the group that first fall when John's brother-in-law, John Stoffel, was killed when a mine on John Polifka's claim caved in. Stoffel's wife and three daughters were forced to leave their claim, unable to live on their own. The Polifka family survived the winter in their sod house and in the Spring of 1909, John cleared 20 more acres of land. He and Helen established a fruitful garden in which they had a bumper crop of watermelon and muskmelon. They purchased some stock, and dug three wells. Things looked promising. But 1910 brought a change. There was very little rain and their crop was extremely poor. The land was parched, and times were difficult. They held out through another winter. But 1911 brought no relief. Their three wells went dry, as well as the watering hole for the cattle. There was no crop. The older children were miserable and lonely, and Helen probably was too, but perhaps kept it to herself. John could see no way that his family could survive another year. In July of that hot, dry summer, John packed up his family, left his claim, and moved back to Tenney. He had tried valiantly to make it work but in the end, Mother Nature was the victor. LaVanche, at age 12, could not have been happier. It had been a lonely, desolate life on the prairie. She liked people, action, fun.

John and Helen's other children were of the more reserved sort. Perhaps as the oldest child, LaVanche felt quite comfortable as a take-charge kind of girl. LaVanche no doubt took note, at age 15, when a handsome, intelligent young man, also age 15, moved to the area with his family in 1914. This young man was Roscoe Gill. Though I am not sure just when it began, LaVanche and Roscoe probably began their courtship not long after Roscoe's family arrived at their home west of Tenney known as the William Cross farm. Roscoe's father, Ed Gill, grew wheat and barley. The family did their trade in both Tenney and Campbell, providing occasions for interaction with both the Tenney and Campbell folks.

LaVanche and Roscoe became "high school sweethearts," apparently dating through much of their teenage years. What that meant in Tenney and Campbell, I'm not sure, but certainly they cut the rug a few times at the Tenney Town Hall, played *500* or **Rook** with the young folks in town, and perhaps there were Sunday afternoon picnics at Ten Mile Lake and jaunts across the Dakota borders to White Rock or Fairmount. I suppose there could have been a lover's leap somewhere in Wilkin County, but I can't imagine where it would be, since it was flat pretty much from there to Wyoming.

Roscoe attended high school in Campbell, as most Tenney kids did, and LaVanche headed to Breckenridge to live with her aunt and uncle, Blanche and Edgar Waite, and attended high school there, though she did not finish. She also attended a few classes at Wahpeton School of Science, but did not obtain a degree. At some point, much to LaVanche's dismay, Roscoe decided to pursue greener pastures with a young woman named Beulah McCoy. I don't know when Roscoe and LaVanche fell out of favor, but presumably this occurred well after Roscoe graduated from high school—so Roscoe and Beulah became an item. Beulah, a local girl, was the daughter of Bertha and Edgar Clark McCoy of Campbell. Edgar was a shopkeeper in Campbell and had the distinction of being Campbell's first undertaker. I suppose this provided Beulah with a better than average station in life in the village of Campbell. At any rate, it is easy to understand why someone would fall in love with a likable, handsome young man such as Roscoe.

In September, 1930, Roscoe and Beulah were married when Roscoe was 30, and Beulah, 25, considered "late in life." After the standard Minnesota honeymoon to the North Shore of Lake Superior, Roscoe and Beulah settled in on Bluff Street in Waukegan, Illinois. They had no children. I have often wondered why, though I suppose it's none of my business. Maybe it had something to do with the "late in life" thing.

It is no secret among family members, and probably most of Tenney and Campbell—and probably Wilkin County—that, as a result of Roscoe's marriage to Beulah, there was no love lost between LaVanche Polifka and Beulah McCoy! At the time of the Tenney Quilt, Roscoe and Beulah would probably have been courting, as they were married two years later. By this time, Roscoe had quite a few life experiences under his belt. He had gone off to serve his country in World War I and safely returned, and had furthered his education and was working as an electrical engineer.

I have to believe that LaVanche had been holding out hope that Roscoe would come to his senses and return to her, so was waiting for him, *just in case.* After all, at the time Roscoe married Beulah, LaVanche had still not married at age 31, somewhat unusual for a woman of her time. Indeed, Roscoe and Beulah's marriage seems to have broken LaVanche's heart, as she waited another 18 more years before she married, at age 48. LaVanche was probably called an "old maid" more than once, an ugly label, but often heard in those days; a condition most likely attributable, in LaVanche's case, to her lost love and her fervent hope for his return.

LaVanche thus focused on her career, affording her professional opportunities that were not always available to women, particularly in a small rural Minnesota town such as Tenney. She began her professional career at the Tenney State Bank in July of 1918, at the age of 19. She would stay there until 1927 or early 1928, just prior to the time when the bank closed its doors.

In the first twenty years of the twentieth century, most of the small villages in Wilkin County had a bank, most of them small businesses with $10,000 or less in capital (Gazette Publications, 1968). James Colehaur served as the cashier at the Tenney Bank in its early years, and William McAlpin, whose father had owned the Farmers' Elevator in town, ran the bank until his death in 1920. At the time of the quilt in 1928, the Tenney Bank was still in operation and Henry Stines ("H. S.") Rose was its president, with clerk LaVanche just recently having left employment. H.S. Rose's name appears on the Tenney Quilt. However, the bank's demise was close at hand, as it was only one year later that the nation's economy turned south after the Stock Market Crash. Many of these small banks, Tenney included, were forced to close their doors. I am not certain of the exact year, but by 1930 it had ceased operating, so the economic conditions of 1929 most likely caused its closure. There were several indications in the Tenney news accounts of 1928 of various visits to the bank by some of its directors, and this could be an indication of the bank's impending closure.

Oral history indicates that many Tenney folks lost "a lot of money" when the Tenney Bank closed. Julius Schendel, president of the First National Bank in Campbell, next door to Tenney, appears to have been a bit more proactive, selling out to First National of Breckenridge before any patron would suffer a loss.

Prior to leaving Tenney, LaVanche had the distinction of being the first woman to serve on the Campbell Township Board, when she became treasurer in 1923, at age 24. She had followed in the footsteps of her father, John Polifka, who had also served on the township board as a young man. Once she left Tenney, LaVanche continued her banking career for about four years at the First National Bank of Wheaton. It was here that LaVanche lived during the time period that the quilt was made, and Wheaton provides the key to several names on the

LaVanche Polifka.

quilt. Names that were previously a mystery to me due to their seeming lack of connection to Tenney proved to be LaVanche's landlord and roommates in Wheaton. She lived in a home owned by Mrs. Gust Ulrich and their daughter Luella, about LaVanche's age, and younger son, Wilbert, each of whose names appears on the quilt. Additionally, the names of four other young professionals, all living with LaVanche and working in Wheaton, appear on the quilt.

After four years at the Wheaton bank, LaVanche moved on to the bank in Sisseton, South Dakota for a few years, and then began a long career as a welfare case worker in 1936, initially at the Wilkin County Courthouse in Breckenridge for six years. In what would be her final career move, LaVanche landed a job as a county welfare worker at the Pope County Courthouse in Glenwood, Minnesota. It is there that LaVanche met Erick John Solvie, the court house custodian and bailiff, eleven years her senior.

LaVanche became a well-respected professional in Glenwood, holding a position normally requiring a college degree. Though not even a high school graduate, she had been so capable in the same type of position in Wilkin County that she was hired in Glenwood without the normal credentials. I have to believe that it was through sheer stubbornness and persistence that LaVanche continually pushed her career forward and landed jobs that other women of her time would perhaps not have pursued. LaVanche and Erick fell in love and were married in 1948. LaVanche was 49, Erick 60.

Erick, previously widowed at a young age, had built a home in Glenwood for his first family that was now a perfect spot for LaVanche and him to live their life together—right across the street from the courthouse in which they both worked. LaVanche retired at age 65, and Erick, not until age 78! LaVanche then set about taking care of Erick as he aged and his health became fragile. It was during my childhood years, the Fifties and Sixties, that I came to know LaVanche and Erick as another set of grandparents. Our family lived in Glenwood, where my father taught English at Glenwood High School. Our home during these years was located right across the street from LaVanche and Erick, providing the opportunity for lots of visiting, and lots of treats for me and my brother and sister. We moved away from Glenwood when I was in elementary school, but visited Glenwood frequently afterwards.

One October evening in 1972, after 24 years of marriage to LaVanche, Erick was struck and killed while walking across a busy street in Glenwood, leaving LaVanche a widow. As a young child myself growing up in Glenwood, that street, Minnesota Avenue, was the imaginary line that marked the boundary of safe passage for a kindergartener on bicycle or on foot, and I was never allowed to navigate that street by myself, except on the way to school when there were school patrol officers on duty. Erick was killed at dusk when a young driver bent down to turn on his headlights. His moment of inattention cost LaVanche the second lost love of her life, and serious injury to another gentleman walking with Erick.

Meanwhile, Roscoe and Beulah lived in Illinois, where Roscoe enjoyed a long and successful career as an electrical engineer with the Public Service Company of Northern Illinois. Roscoe lost his wife only one year before LaVanche lost Erick. Roscoe began spending his winters in Bradenton, Florida in his retirement, and LaVanche continued to live alone in Glenwood. Rumor has it that LaVanche's childhood friend from Tenney, Elsie Hamann, put a bug in LaVanche's ear that Beulah had passed away, and Roscoe was therefore single again. And Roscoe had also gotten the word through his connections back home in Minnesota that LaVanche was now widowed.

Jackpot!

Roscoe sent a letter of condolence to LaVanche, and they resumed a courtship suspended some 60 years earlier. The once-teenage sweethearts were married the very next July, both at age 74. LaVanche had been a loving and dedicated wife to her beloved Erick and had treated his family as her own. But what joy she must have felt on that day in 1973 when she married her first love and became Mrs. Roscoe Gill.

They married quietly, and lived together in what had been LaVanche and Erick's home in Glenwood. Love had come full circle for LaVanche and Roscoe. They had no doubt found in each other a certain familiarity, comfort, and common history at a time when they most needed it. They acted like a couple of lovebirds, amusing to 17-year-old me, who naively believed that falling in love was reserved for young people such as myself and my pimple-faced adolescent friends.

Roscoe took exceedingly good care of his long lost sweetheart. He was the sweet and attentive balance to LaVanche's somewhat ornery demeanor at times in her later life. I say that, however, with a sense of immeasurable affection for this lovable great aunt of mine who had a heart of gold. She had a kind, generous and totally hilarious spirit under that sometimes-ornery exterior.

Chapter Two of LaVanche and Roscoe's love story lasted 13 years when, in 1986, Roscoe died of pneumonia following surgery. An image seared into my memory has as its backdrop the Riverside Cemetery in tiny Campbell, Minnesota where, some 70 years earlier, two young teenage kids fell in love. Against this backdrop, 86-year-old LaVanche, racked with sobs and inconsolable, is caressing the casket of her first love, Roscoe Gill.

Streaking

One cannot reminisce about LaVanche's later years without bringing up an incident that still moves various family members to fits of laughter to the point of tears. In LaVanche's very last years as she was slowly losing her physical and mental capabilities, she lived in a nursing home near our home in west central Minnesota. She was known and loved at that facility as a witty woman who had on occasion been known for her snappy comebacks.

Now at age 98, moving fast was out of the question for LaVanche. On one particular day, she was navigating the hallway with her walker at the speed of molasses, on her way to lunch or some other activity. Seemingly without major provocation, her drawers—both layers—unceremoniously slipped from the confines of her body, right down to her ankles, revealing what must have been a rather interesting sight approaching her from the "rear", so to speak.

A nurse's aide approached her from behind and said, stifling a grin, "LaVanche! What are you doing? You lost your pants!" Without a moment's hesitation, LaVanche responded, "I'm streaking."

* * *

LaVanche died at that nursing home at age 99, in March, 1998. If she had only had a clue that, in two months, she would have celebrated her 100th birthday, I'm sure she would have figured out a way to make that happen.

CHAPTER 4

- *The Home Makers* -

Lizzie

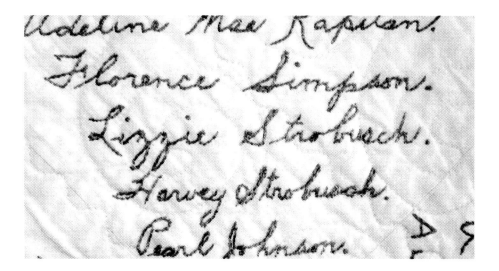

Lizzie Strobusch—pronounced "Straw Bush"—was a 54-year-old widow living with her son, Harvey, in a little bungalow in South Minneapolis in 1928. Lizzie's story begins and ends in places far from Tenney, but is woven into the fabric of our little prairie town. Lizzie had left the family farm in Tenney to move to Minneapolis just four years prior to the Tenney Quilt, in 1924, but still felt very much a part of Tenney and wanted to be represented on the quilt.

Lizzie Pasewald was born in 1874 in West Germany in an area then known as Prussia, and emigrated to the United States in 1879 as a five-year-old. The family initially settled in Watertown, Wisconsin, part of Dodge County. There was a large settlement of German immigrants in Dodge County, many of whom eventually made their way to the Tenney area. Oral history indicates that there were several families who knew each other in this part of Wisconsin who came west to Tenney at about the same time, with many family members and friends and succeeding generations following them to the area.

My ancestors, the Polifkas and Readys, were in that group, as were the Strobusch, Voss, Kuentzel, Pithey, and Reinhard families, among others. While living in Wisconsin, Lizzie Pasewald and her family were friends with the Strobusch family, who had arrived from Germany in 1869. It was here in Wisconsin that Lizzie and her future husband, Herman Strobusch, became acquainted, though they would have been children at the time. The Strobusch family—father Carl, mother Henrietta, Carl's parents, and three children including Herman, left Wisconsin and moved to the Tenney area in 1881. As the oldest son, Herman was expected to have a hand in the farming operation.

Lizzie came to the Tenney in 1898, presumably to marry Herman, as there is no indication of any of Lizzie's other family members in Tenney or the surrounding area at any time. They were married that same year. It could be that Herman traveled to Watertown to marry Lizzie and bring her back home to Tenney. Up to that point, Herman had lived with his family on the Strobusch farm southwest of Tenney but, once married, moved from the farm and built the home in which my great grandfather and grandmother would live in later years. Though a quiet and unassuming person, Lizzie made many friends in Tenney. She and Herman attended the Tenney Church and Lizzie found meaningful activity and companionship in Tenney's social network as well as comfort in the German heritage of most of its people. Gertie Kapitan became a trusted friend, a person with whom Lizzie would correspond for several years after Lizzie left Tenney. Herman still worked on the family farm, but also used his carpentry skills, both in community construction projects, as well as in building their home in Tenney. Lizzie and Herman sadly lost a baby boy at birth in 1901, and one year later, Lizzie gave birth to another son, Harvey, who would turn out to be Lizzie's last child. With no immediate family in the area, the camaraderie of friends who had similar backgrounds and customs provided the comfort that she needed. A common history, beginning in Germany for most Tenney folks, provided a sense of belonging and camaraderie for many first- and second-generation immigrants on the Minnesota prairie. This camaraderie, as previously mentioned, began for many Tenney families in Wisconsin.

The State of Wisconsin was heavily promoted to Germans while they were still in Germany. Wisconsin had its own State Commissioner of Immigration who distributed nearly 30,000 pamphlets in Germany to potential residents about Wisconsin's soil and climate (Rippley, 1989). This person not only sought out people to settle in Wisconsin, but provided services to them once they arrived, such as helping them through land procurement, citizenship, and other bureaucratic processes that often seemed complicated and frightening to new immigrants, particularly when they did not speak English. Pamphlets not only praised the fertility of the soil, but also of the manufacturing potential in America, the need for good strong men to build railroads and cut down forests, and even the extraordinary healing powers of the climate for ailments such as Tuberculosis and pulmonary diseases! Wisconsin also had liberal land policies, important to the Germans, who as a people placed a great value on land ownership. Federal acreage was sold to immigrants at the minimum price allowed by the government, $1.25 per acre (Rippley, 1989). Inheritance laws in Germany in effect in the mid-nineteenth century restricted inheritance of family land to the eldest son and prevented division of that land to younger siblings. Land was simply becoming scarce and thus more expensive, making the plentiful land in America very appealing. When one considered the heavy "recruiting" to come to Wisconsin, along with the fact that Wisconsin was very similar in appearance to Germany, it is no wonder that many German emigrants set their sights on that state.

Families then moved further and further west with each succeeding generation or when brave souls ventured to places where they had heard more land was available. Almost 5.6 million Germans found their way to the United States between 1820 and 1930 (Conzen, 2003) with the flow stopped only when the Great Depression began and more restrictive U.S. immigration policies were put into practice. So many German immigrants—and others, of course—came to America through "chain migration," i.e., family members bringing or persuading relatives and friends, who in turn brought or persuaded other relatives and friends, generation after generation. Chain migration has evolved into a somewhat controversial topic in the modern immigration debate regarding automatic family reunification, in which foreigners are eligible for a visa because of a relative who lives in the United States.

The Strobusch family farm in Tenney, from which Herman had moved in order to live in town with Lizzie, was located adjacent to the Pleasant Hill Cemetery. The farm had been homesteaded when Strobusches came to Wilkin County from Wisconsin in 1881. In fact, it was the Strobusch family who donated the small plot of land for the Pleasant Hill Church, to be located next to the cemetery, in 1901, three years after Herman and Lizzie's marriage, and Herman was one of the three primary builders of that church.

So Lizzie and Herman began their married life in their modest home on the southwest corner of town. Lizzie's life would soon take a turn that she certainly would not have anticipated, and which would point her life in a direction away from the little village of Tenney. Apparently Lizzie's husband Herman had chronic nephritis (kidney disease), and died from this illness in 1913 at the very young age of 46. Given the characteristics of such a disease, Herman probably had an extended period of time up until his death during which he was ill. This meant that Herman and Lizzie would have had a relatively short time to just live a normal married life, perhaps not even ten years. During his illness, Lizzie would not only have had the responsibilities of taking care of the household, but also caring for her husband and perhaps contributing something toward the family income such as taking in laundry, sewing, or other domestic tasks. Having come to the area alone to marry Herman and thus having no other immediate family in the area other than her son, Lizzie certainly must have had a difficult time adjusting to the unexpected burden and loneliness of widowhood. She had had her share of tragedy in her young life, first with the lost of their newborn son and now, her young husband. However, Lizzie doted on her other son, Harvey, who attended the Tenney School and to Lizzie's pride and delight was a bright and promising student. Harvey graduated from the eighth grade at the Tenney School and moved in with a family in Elbow Lake High to attend high school two years after his father's death.

There is a four-year span between the time that Herman died and when Lizzie sold her house to my great grandfather and grandmother, John and Helen Polifka, in 1917. At some point Lizzie moved out to the Strobusch family farm, perhaps due to the fact that she was now completely alone, with Herman deceased and Harvey boarding in Elbow Lake while attending high school. Lizzie may have moved out to the Strobusch farm with her in-laws immediately after Herman's death, or she may have stayed in town for those four years. In any case, the 1920 census shows Lizzie and son Harvey living on the family farm, in a separate home, perhaps with young Harvey working on the farm to help support himself and Lizzie. Harvey had recently graduated from Elbow Lake High School as valedictorian of his class of 1919.

Lizzie, though having been raised on a farm, now had to adjust from town life to farm life, which at the time was not an easy transition. Her aging parents-in-law, Carl and Henrietta Strobusch had, by this time, handed over the operation of the farm to sons Fred and William. When they first came to Tenney to claim a homestead, times were very tough out on the prairie. There was little automation and convenience in the activities of daily life, and these things were slow to improve. A family member reports that the only fuel the family had for cooking was twisted hay, cane break from the river, and buffalo chips (Wilkin County Historical Society, 1977). Farm wives such as Lizzie and her mother-in-law, Henrietta, were the cornerstones of rural farm families. These strong, steadfast women of the early twentieth century took care of their families as well as taking care of the cooking, baking bread, mending, and so much more. They would have been doing laundry by hand using a scrubbing board and portable hand-operated wringer. No electricity, no running water, no sewer. Wash water had to be heated in a copper boiler. They would have tended the wood stove and carried water from the outside well into their kitchens. The sheer physical nature of the farm wife's work was daunting. And their work was not confined to the inside of the house. Women were often in charge of the milking and very often did field work. At butchering time, they prepared the meat for curing or scalding down, and made soap out of the waste fats. They were usually the caretakers and cultivators of the family garden, and sometimes sold produce and eggs to supplement an otherwise limited farm income. In Lizzie's case, after Herman's death, it could be that this was one of her few sources of income. She most likely had chickens. In many families, the egg money was very often the "woman's money", designated for things such as birthday presents, Christmas presents, or church donations, those things considered at that time to be in the women's realm. As the wooden egg cases became full, they were sometimes sent to the A.N. Larson Store in town along with the cream delivery.

The Strobusches raised wheat, as did most farmers in that part of the Red River Valley at the turn of the century (Blegen, 1938). During World War I, the U.S. Government sent the message that food would win the war. That logic and motivation worked fine during the World War I years, but after the war, too much food was being produced and as a result, crop prices fell. So to make money at the lower prices, each farmer had to grow more. And with the overabundance of wheat and lack of diversification in Wilkin County, the productivity of the farm land declined. Murray postulates that the most important reason for the difficulties and shortcomings of Red River agriculture was the attitude of valley farmers toward diversification (Murray, 1967). In a nutshell, diversification was met with much resistance.

In the very tough 1920s and 30s, many small farmers simply had to give up. They couldn't afford the new machinery, yet could not keep going without them. Often served by a single railroad and located a long distance either from their source of supplies or their market, transportation and fuel costs were simply beyond their ability to pay. Their fields were taken over by the larger farmers who *could* keep up. According to the Breckenridge Gazette article in December, 1928, citing the 1925 census figures, "Wilkin County has the distinction of having the largest average size farms of any county in Minnesota, namely 320.4 acres. This is more than double the average sized farm of Minnesota, which is 159.7 acres." (***Breckenridge Gazette,***

12/12/1928, p 1). Young people of German immigrant families in southern Wilkin County were indoctrinated with the premise that land was the finest form of wealth and the greatest indicator of success. They were told to invest in land. As parents spoke to their children about their ancestors, it was those ancestors' ability to purchase and improve the land that defined their success. The expression "to lose the farm" grew out of the ridicule and shame that came with doing just that. So many immigrants, whether German or otherwise, came to this country because of the value they placed on land ownership.

Often families were large enough that the sons could help in the operation, with extra help needed only during threshing time. If they needed laborers, they were not hard to find, particularly in the railroad towns. Floyd Doty, a Wilkin County resident, reports that many young men would hop off the train in a town and ask which farmers were in need of workers. In the late 1920s and early 1930s, they worked "for their board and room and a little tobacco and clothes." In the Depression years, they worked for $15 per month plus board (Wilkin County Historical Society, 1977)

Bert Huse, a local farmer, auctioneer, and Wilkin County Commissioner in 1929 was a very progressive farmer in the area, one of the first farmers in Wilkin County to understand the need to diversify his operation beyond the production of small grains. In the 1928 time frame, he bought livestock, and then began to grow crops to feed his herds. Though Wilkin County was previously thought to be too far north to grow corn, Mr. Huse brought in corn seed from Iowa, and was credited for introducing it in the area. Not only that, but he had owned his own threshing rig, which he used to thresh his own grain, as well as that of others. As a result of his foresight and his willingness to diversify his farming operation, he was very successful. Many were not. J.W. Noffsinger farmed south east of Campbell and was quite successful in producing honey and muskmelons at the turn of the century, certainly not common agricultural products of the time. By 1925, nearly every farm had a tractor, some of which even had rubber tires! The combine would not be introduced until the early 1930s, the same time period during which farmers suffered miserably from drought, dust storms, and grasshoppers.

Lizzie's son Harvey was a very bright young man, and after graduating from a successful high school career at Elbow Lake High School, apparently did not have the passion for farming the land to pursue life on the Strobusch family farm, or perhaps did not have the option, as the Strobusch family was very large and his uncles would have been running the farm at that time. Harvey landed in Minneapolis three years after high school graduation, in 1922, initially working as a salesman at the Business Letter Company. Lizzie left her Tenney farm home in 1924 to join Harvey in Minneapolis, never to return, yet obviously keeping in contact, as her name appeared on the Tenney Quilt four years later. Lizzie maintained and valued her friendship with Gertie long distance, as Gertie and her husband Matt received a 25th anniversary card from Lizzie thirteen years after Lizzie had left the Tenney area.

While living in Minneapolis, Lizzie's son Harvey appeared to have a successful sales career. He worked for companies which were eventually bought by Stor-Enso, a multinational company that manufactures paper and wood products. Over a 12-year period of time, he was promoted to various positions in the Business Envelope Company, Hudson Manufacturing, Ontario Paper Company, and The Insulite Company. In August, 1930, when he was employed by the Insulite Company, Harvey married Pearl Elna Johnson, the daughter of August Johnson of Chisago County, Minnesota, a Swedish stronghold that just happens to be the home of my own Swedish immigrant ancestors. Pearl's name appears on the Tenney Quilt right next to Lizzie and Harvey in 1928, so we know Harvey and Pearl had at least a two-year courtship. Pearl, at the time of her marriage at age 24, had worked for several years as a typist and clerk at a farm implement dealer in Minneapolis.

During this entire time, since 1924, Lizzie lived with Harvey in his bungalow on 15th Avenue South in Minneapolis. Lizzie and her son were very close, having survived together as a family of two since 1913 without husband and father, Herman. For the entire time that Lizzie lived in Minneapolis with Harvey, she was not employed outside of her home, so I am presuming that she worked at home, taking care of the cooking, mending, and cleaning for Harvey and herself. The work ethic of Lizzie the farm wife continued in her role as mother and house mate to Harvey. Lizzie continued to live with Harvey and Pearl after their marriage, and four years later, in 1934, all three moved to San Mateo County, California. I am assuming that this move was precipitated by a promotion or job offer for Harvey, but I was never able to determine this.

Lizzie's life ended there, in California, in 1944, far away from her humble beginnings on a different side of the world. Lizzie's immigrant journey took her from Eastern Europe, to Canada, then on to Watertown, Wisconsin; Tenney, Minnesota; and finally, to San Mateo County, California, her final resting place. There are many holes in Lizzie's life story. And I have not been able to understand her life and capture her personality through the loving words and reminiscences of a grandchild or niece or someone who tasted her homemade bread, or heard her stories, or held her gnarled hand in theirs. What I do know is that Lizzie's story is worth telling. Her legacy is one of strength, faith to step forward into the unknown, and most of all, loving devotion to her only surviving child. She first left behind her family in Germany as she took her mother's hand and stepped on to a boat that would carry their small family to an unfamiliar and foreign land. She then left the comfort of her family in Wisconsin in order to move to the unknown frontier of Tenney, Minnesota, to start a new life with Herman. Then, when tragedy struck only a decade later and Lizzie had no one but her 11-year-old son, Lizzie's attention turned to providing the best life possible for him and nurturing his talents in order to assure he grew up happy and successful. Harvey returned the favor when, after obtaining a good-paying job and a home in the city, he called for his mother to join him in chasing his dreams.

Harvey, like his father, died at a relatively young age, 56, fourteen years after his mother, in California where, together, they are buried. A fitting scenario for a mother and her son whose foundation as a family of two was firmly planted in the little prairie town of Tenney, Minnesota.

Gertie

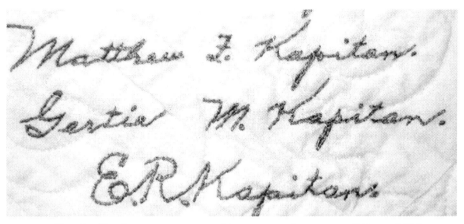

Gertie Kapitan was a true Tenney native, one of five children born to Tenney farmers, Philip and Diana Reinhard, in 1892, and at the time of the Tenney Quilt in 1928 was a 36-year-old mother of eight children.

Gertie's father Philip came as an 18-year-old from Dodge County, Wisconsin like so many others in Tenney after hearing about the fertile Red River Valley soil in the Tenney area. Philip married Diana Main in 1889, at which time they began a family and a successful farming operation in rural Tenney. The Reinhards were popular, sociable people with many friends. Diana was involved in many community activities, while Philip played on the town baseball team. Their children included sons Orlando ("Lanny"), and Irvin, who both lived to adulthood and Grant, who died in infancy; and daughters Gertie and Mae. Gertie, an outgoing, friendly sort, was the only child of Philip and Diana to stay in Tenney and, as it turned out, made it her home for her entire married life.

Gertie was deeply involved in the Tenney Church. Due to Tenney's pint-sized population, most residents attended the same church. That's just the way it was in many of the small villages in Wilkin County; these communities could rarely support more than one church. As a result, they tended to be church-centered communities. Now, that doesn't necessarily mean that Tenney was made up only of God-fearing, pious people whose actions were determined solely by their religious beliefs. However, it does mean that church activities and church holidays often became community-wide celebrations and involved all generations—grandparents, parents, children. On the occasion of the church's annual ice cream social, for example, most townspeople were involved, either as workers or as guests. Children were recruited to turn the handles of the many ice cream freezers spread about the church's front yard, and were then allowed to lick the paddles of the freezers as a reward when the ice cream was ready. In Tenney, the standard church social functions were held in the church's social hall, but many of the larger church events were in the Town Hall and became community-wide events. The "church women's" network extended well beyond Sunday morning services, and Christian Aid and mission societies and Ladies Aid became synonymous with the town's social network for women.

Church was important. Amy Richardson, one of Tenney's long-time and most beloved residents and a good friend of Gertie's, loved her church and attended every week, no matter what. The Richardsons lived within sight distance of town, on a farm just across the field north of town. In the winter time, if the roads were blocked, Amy would ask Jack to hook up the "honey wagon," a slightly more delicate name for what most of us know as the manure spreader. Amy would load up the kids and off they would go, with Jack driving the tractor, pulling Amy and the kids on the manure spreader. You do what you gotta do, by golly.

In 1928 in Tenney, a core group of women was quite active in the "Ladies Aid" group which met monthly. This group included—among others, I'm sure—Gertie Kapitan, Amy Richardson, Mary Gore, Minnie Wittman, Florence Dawson, Linda Larson, Marie Moon, and Cora Hamann. Several women from Taylor Township also came in to town including Rose Reiss, Bessie Briggs, and Mrs. Robert Johnston. Mind you, I wouldn't call her "Mrs. Robert Johnston" if I knew her first name! It was standard etiquette at the time, but my 21st century mentality has trouble identifying a woman solely by her husband's first and last name. The women took turns hosting the monthly gathering, which generally included a short business meeting with afternoon coffee, sometimes even extending to the evening meal time. Sometimes the group met in homes; sometimes in the Church's social hall. Whatever the format or the topic, food was always involved. The Ladies Aid group represented all age groups but in 1928, the worker bees seemed to be mostly women in their thirties and forties, precisely where our Gertie Kapitan fell.

Gertie's granddaughter Barbara, who often accompanied her grandma to Ladies Aid meetings as a child, recalls with great pleasure and comfort three distinct aromas from those meetings—coffee, homemade pickles, and "women." Whether we realize it or not, we all take pleasure in the comfortable, familiar scents of those people who are close to us, and our grandmas are right at the top of the list. Whether it's the smell of her powder, the freshness of her clothesline-dried house dress, the smell of baked goods, coffee, or just an un-identified "grandma" scent, some primal instinct within us memorizes the comfort of those aromas. I recall those same things about my own grandmas and their houses, and it also works in the opposite genera-tional direction. As a grandma myself, there is little in the world bet-ter than burying my nose into my granddaughter's little face or neck and memorizing the softness and aroma. It is always the last thing I do when I know I won't see her for awhile.

Often the Ladies Aid group spent their meeting time planning events to raise money for various items needed at the church or to help the minister and his family. The Ladies Aid was quite active in 1928. During the summer months, they hosted a Saturday evening ice cream and pie social at the Town Hall as a fund raiser. Additionally, Tenney was busy this early summer of 1928 preparing the parsonage for the Roser family to arrive in early July. The Ladies Aid took charge of sprucing up the home and planting a garden for the minister's fam-ily. Rev. Roser was to replace Rev. Robert Reinhart, who had left quite a while earlier, a time frame I am guessing to be several months. Ministers were often shared among the area churches during the times when the churches were between full-time clergymen, so Tenney's citizens were anxiously awaiting the arrival of the Roser family. That November, the Ladies Aid hosted a "Ladies Aid Sale and Supper," also at the Town Hall, which netted "a very satisfying" $105.75.

The Taylor Evangelical Church, just outside of Tenney in Taylor Township, had a "Women's Missionary Aid Society" which was also quite active in 1928. The group seemed to have a bit of influence with our Gertie Kapitan, as their meetings are mentioned frequently in the local gossip column. Members of this club included Jane Irvine, Mary Kuentzel, her daughter-in-law Agnes Kuentzel, and Emma Propp, among others. At one mission society meeting in February of 1928, there were 68 people present, including 19 men. The men apparently spent the afternoon playing *Rook* while the women conducted their business, and then socialized. A total of $36 was taken in for the Missionary Aid Society, an amount considered to be a very successful afternoon's worth of benevolence. Rev. J. Haueter was pastor at the Taylor Church at this time, a gentleman whose dental activities were also chronicled in the local news. Thanks to Gertie Kapitan's reporting we know that one night in January, 1928, "Rev Haueter had dental work done at Elbow Lake Sunday night between trains." Everyone apparently was interested in such news!

Another church that has significant role in Tenney's history is the "Frieden Church," also known as the "Pleasant Hill Church." Anyone familiar with Tenney would simply know it in later years as the "social hall." The church received title from the Strobusch family to a half acre of land in 1901 on a ridge known as "Pleasant Hill." The "hill" is located about a mile and a half east of the Bois de Sioux River, which forms the boundary between Minnesota and North Dakota. Only in the Red River Valley of Wilkin County would such a bump in the ground be considered a "hill," but that's beside the point. The land for the church was located across the road from the Pleasant Hill Cemetery which had been established ten years prior in order to bury the early pioneers who lived in the immediate area but had no church. The road that ran between the church and the cemetery happened to be the boundary between Wilkin County and Traverse County.

The Pleasant Hill Church initially served as an Evangelical Lutheran Church. Immigrants from northern and western Germany, such as those who settled in Tenney, were often Lutheran, whereas those from the southern and eastern regions of Germany tended to be Catholic (Conzen, 2003). German Lutherans were as prominent as the German Catholics, but did not have as unified a presence in Minnesota because of the synodical divisions within the Lutheran Church. This created multiple layers of division within immigrant groups in the German Lutheran Church. German Lutherans were thus separated from other Lutheran groups not only by synods, but also because of their German heritage and language. I am very familiar with the establishment of churches by separate immigrant groups. In my own town of New London, Minnesota, I am a member of a Lutheran Church which was the result of a merger between a Norwegian Lutheran and Swedish Lutheran congregation—a merger that, in 1962, created a brouhaha that apparently rivaled the magnitude of the Great Flood.

After its use as a Lutheran church, the Frieden Church became affiliated with the United Brethren, and then served for two years as a Church of the Nazarene. After its 35-year life as a house of worship, its doors were closed and it stood empty for a number of years. The little country church was then sold to the Tenney Church for a sum of one hundred dollars and moved into the Village of Tenney in 1940, where it stands today, across the street from the Tenney Church. The building served as the Tenney Church's "social hall" from that point forward, and the hundred dollars gained in the sale of the church was given to the Pleasant Hill Cemetery for perpetual care.

The farm wives and homemakers were the most likely to be involved in the women's organizations and benevolence activities in the 1920s in Tenney. Women were seen as "more sensitive" than men, and it was their duty to improve not only their homes, but their communities and the outside world as well. Caring for the community was considered to be part of the women's sphere, an extension of the mothering and housekeeping that women, from a societal viewpoint, did exceedingly well. Women's experience as housekeepers and caretakers in the home; nurturers for the sick, aged and children; and food purchasers and preparers spilled over into their roles in women's organizations. By viewing the community or the region as a home, women were able to be involved in the community without arousing as much opposition as if they were so audacious as to own a business, run for public office, or openly express an opinion on a civic matter.

Other women's organizations that were in existence during this period of time, but not in the immediate Tenney area to my knowledge, were the National Parent-Teacher Association, the Pythian Sisters, and Eastern Star. I would have put the Women's Christian Temperance Union (WCTU) on this list until recently when I learned that this group did indeed have a presence in the Tenney area, just not right in the Village of Tenney. The WCTU grew to be the largest women's organization in the later nineteenth century and a major national political force. By 1907, the organization boasted 350,000 members across the nation (Hedges/Ferraro 15), and dealt with a broad range of women's issues such as prohibition, child welfare, women's working conditions, women's health, equal pay for equal work, and international peace (Bingham 438). Though there was not an active chapter right in town, the women of Tenney would certainly have been exposed to it and been familiar with it, since I discovered that WCTU meetings were held in the school building at the Elliot railroad station just six miles east of Tenney during this time period. I am increasingly suspicious, however, that there may have been a greater presence than I have been able to unearth. I learned that Jennie Waite, a Tenney pioneer married to Thomas B. ("T.B.") Waite, was a member of the WCTU. Though they lived, in their younger years, on a farm west of Tenney, Jennie lived right in Tenney, next to the parsonage, at one time. Perhaps there was a group of women in town who were involved in the organization, but Gertie Kapitan, in her role as rural correspondent, chose not to cover their activities, either due to her opposition or her lack of involvement in the organization. Newspapers and radio would have covered the activities of this group, and there may also have been a WCTU chapter in Breckenridge. With the colors of the WCTU being blue and white, I have pondered once or twice whether or not the distinct blue and white color scheme of the Tenney Quilt could possibly have been a reflection of the Tenney women's affiliation with the organization, but I have found no evidence that the organization had a significant presence or importance right in Tenney or Campbell.

There was little opportunity for women to have meaningful employment in Tenney. Not unlike the remainder of the country, women's work tended toward unwaged family work or low-waged work with little status or influence, though there were a few exceptions, some of which are mentioned by way of the life stories told in this book. Another exception would be the position of Postmaster ("Postmistress"), which was held by four different women over the course of Tenney's history: Alice Cook, Lillie Scott, Elizabeth Parks, and Opal Hardie. In 1928, Elizabeth Parks was the Postmistress.

There was a mixture of men and women who held this Postmaster/mistress position through the years, with the men generally served as the rural carriers. My family, the Polifkas, had lots of connections with the U.S. Postal Service in Tenney's early years. My great grandfather, John Polifka, was Tenney's first Postmaster and was responsible for setting up the original 26-mile rural mail route, which was subsequently delivered by his brother-in-law, Ray Gore. The next rural mail carrier was John Polifka's brother, Albert Polifka. Then John Polifka himself served as the rural carrier. And John's son, Clifford Polifka, who ran the local tavern, was the substitute carrier for several decades. Once the Polifkas had run out, Cecil Davidson and Al Manthie served next in line as Tenney's rural mail carriers. Al Manthie was "Mr. Tenney" if there ever was someone who deserved the title. Al and his wife, Lou Ida, were two of the very last hold-outs among the long-timers to live in Tenney. Al served as village clerk for over 40 years, taking care of the town's books, the Village Hall, and the Fire Hall, and lovingly stood watch over Tenney until his death in 1998. In 1972, the rural route was consolidated with that of Fairmount, North Dakota, just across the border.

So, though the rural mail route was handled primarily by men, several women throughout Tenney's history played an active part in the operation of the Tenney Post Office. In 1928, because of the general unavailability and lack of acceptance of women working in paying jobs outside of the home, women sought involvement in women's groups both as a social outlet and as a means of helping the community and even larger causes. Through this type of companionship and camaraderie, women shared feelings, helped each other, strengthened the bonds in their community, and strengthened their own sense of purpose at a time when the world was all about men. Additionally, as first- and second-generation immigrants, these groups served as a means of finding the support of other compatriots who had a common history, similar religious background, and were interested in the same foods and the same traditions.

Women's groups of this era tended to focus on one of two areas, reform activity or benevolence activity. Those in Tenney focused primarily on the latter. In 1928, four separate women's groups were quite active in Tenney: (1) The Women's Missionary Aid Society, based at Taylor Church; (2) the Ladies Aid, based at the Tenney Church; (3) "The Club," a group of Tenney women whose original purpose was as a time to get together with other women and mend clothing and create other handiwork (sometimes referred to as "the Mending Club"); and (4) the Royal Neighbors. A few years later, in the early Thirties, a group of women formed the "Tenney Home Management Club," and I'm quite sure there were other women's groups which met in the town's later history. These women's groups in the Twenties focused primarily on relationships and issues within their own town, with the Ladies Aid involvement in the Tenney fundraising quilt as a prime example. The women's groups that focused on reform activity, typically in the larger metropolitan areas, tended to have members that held slightly higher positions on the social ladder, and thus had more resources to be concerned with issues beyond their own families.

The Royal Neighbors had a strong presence in Tenney. The organization had originally been formed as an auxiliary to the Modern Woodmen of America, a fraternal men's organization. It later reorganized as a social organization, but maintained the constitution, articles of incorporation, and many of the same club rituals as the original organization. The name *Royal Neighbors of America* was derived from Proverbs 27:10, "For better is a neighbor that is near than a brother that is far." The word "royal" was added to emphasize the nobility of their work (Royal Neighbors of America, 2007). The organization stressed the values most important to pioneering women who formed the group in the late nineteenth century: *faith, unselfishness, courage, endurance, modesty,* and *morality* (Royal Neighbors of America, 2007). The Royal Neighbors "camp" in Tenney was formed in 1897 and Emma Ready, my great great grandmother, was a charter member, establishing the tradition which was followed in her family by two succeeding generations. From its onset, the organization focused primarily on benevolence within the community, as well as social engagement and mutual support. However, even in Tenney, the organization did occasionally act on wider issues important to women in the early twentieth century such as suffrage, life insurance for women, child labor, and help for the poor. But for the most part, in Tenney, as in so many of the other rural Midwestern communities of the time, some of these more global issues were not as critical as in the metropolitan areas because people within the community took care of each other and, for example, simply didn't have to worry about help for the poor. They looked after their own poor.

In Tenney, the Royal Neighbors met regularly, sometimes in conjunction with an equally active Royal Neighbors camp in Campbell. I was tickled to learn that purple had been chosen as their club's color. I could not help making the connection between today's "Red Hat Society," whose colors are red and purple, and its inspiration, the poem known by most people as *When I Am Old, I Shall Wear Purple* (actual title, *Warning,* by Jenny Joseph). It speaks of growing old in a delightfully outrageous manner—wearing purple clothing with a red hat, eating three pounds of sausage in one sitting, wearing terrible shirts, spending one's pension on brandy and summer gloves,

Tenney's Royal Neighbors, circa 1920.

pressing alarm bells, and hoarding pens and pencils and storing them in boxes (Joseph, Warning: When I Am Old I Shall Wear Purple, 2001). I personally find the poem quite appealing, especially the last few lines which state that the author is going to practice these things now so that it's not such a shock to her friends and family when she gets old. I have to admit that I have come to a point in my life, at age 51, where, if I feel like eating three pounds of sausage in one sitting, and hoarding pens and pencils in a box in my closet—well—that's what I'm going to do. So be it! In an old scrapbook of my grandmother's I saw a photo of several Tenney women sitting on a row of chairs with their fancy hats in front of the Town Hall, and I wonder if that might have been the Royal Neighbors, and I would like to think that at least one of those hats was purple!

The Royal Neighbors followed the established rituals of the organization such as a rather elaborate initiation of new members, and the ceremonial election of the various positions such as Oracle and Vice-Oracle (leaders), Chancellor, Marshal, Sentinels, and others. Group meetings were steeped with rituals, symbolism, and pomp and circumstance, closely followed by heavy doses of food and fellowship.

Royal Neighbor activities abounded in 1928 in Tenney. Installation of new officers, with families in attendance at the meeting, occurred in January. The meeting was followed by a "big feed consisting of scalloped oysters, celery, buns, fruit salad, cake and coffee." In February, the group held the Royal Neighbors Masquerade Ball, complete with masks, costumes, and prizes, at the Tenney Town Hall. The annual Royal Neighbors picnic was at Ten Mile Lake in June. A meeting in October was dedicated to organizing a district convention, and in December, new members Agnes Pithey, Mary Belle Pithey, Hattie "Hats" Shaffer, and Rose O'Laughlin were initiated in a lavish ceremony, followed by a "very nice supper" served by the old members to the new. The Town Hall, "daintily trimmed in their colors purple," was the site of the New Year's Night carnival dance. Russell O'Laughlin, talented local musician, stepped in and played the piano for the dance when the orchestra from Lidgerwood, North Dakota was involved in an automobile accident on the way to its gig in Tenney.

Besides all the ceremonial and social activities, Tenney's Royal Neighbors typically attended funerals of other Royal Neighbor members as a group and served refreshments to the relatives at their home. My grandmother, Audrey Larson, and great grandmother, Helen Polifka, were active members of this organization, as well as a host of other local women—Belle Gore, Rose Durner, Diana Reinhard, Gertie Kapitan, Malissa Moon, Amy Richardson, Florence Dawson, Elizabeth Parks, Minnie Wittman, and Madge Dawson, to name just a few. These women represented all ages, as apparently once a woman joined, she stayed awhile—like perhaps a lifetime. Multiple generations of women from one family were often members.

The formality of the rituals of the organization became abundantly clear as I read a "proclamation" sent to my grandmother, a Royal Neighbor, at the occasion of the death of her stepson in 1931:

> "Whereas, Divine Providence has bereaved Neighbor Audrey Larson of her stepson, Andrew Larson. Florence Camp, No. 1012, desiring to express its sympathy, decrees the following resolutions: Be it therefore resolved, that, we the officers and members of this Camp, extend our heartfelt sympathy to Neighbor Audrey Larson in her bereavement. Be it further resolved, that a copy of these resolutions be presented to Audrey Larson and a copy be spread upon the records of this Camp." (Signed) ***Hattie Shaffer, Florence Dawson, and Rose O'Laughlin.***

I have not been able to adequately identify the emotions I felt when reading this expression of condolence enough to explain them, but they lie somewhere in the vast area between fascination, repulsion, humor, and respect.

An example in which Tenney did extend its benevolence well beyond the city limits occurred in October, 1928, when Wilkin County was asked to commit $200 to the Red Cross to help sufferers of the recent hurricane in Florida and "Porto" Rico. Each small town in Wilkin County was expected to be involved, as dictated by the Red Cross county official. Tenney rose to the occasion, most likely under the coordination of Gertie Kapitan, with a total contribution of twelve dollars and twenty-five cents, thanks to a list of 20 donors who each gave 50 cents. One citizen, Estella Gill, a local farmer's wife, gave a very generous two dollars. It was clear that the business people in town were asked for contributions and thus appear on the list of contributors in the Breckenridge newspaper: Louie Wittman (local auto repairman), Ida Klugman (general store owner), Clifford Polifka (tavern owner), Janice Johnson and Octavia Askegaard (local school teachers), George Dopp (manager of local shipping association), Matt Kapitan (railroad station agent), and the list goes on. Gertie Kapitan served on the county's Red Cross Committee for twenty years and was passionate about its causes, so she no doubt had a hand in coordinating the collection of these donations. As a woman of modest means, Gertie must have felt very important and privileged to be the Wilkin County delegate to the American Red Cross Midwestern Area Conference in St. Paul on more than one occasion.

The Red Cross was also involved in the eradication of Tuberculosis during this time period, with several Red Cross drives held for that purpose in the area. My grandfather A.N.'s first wife succumbed to this disease while living in Tenney in 1929. Tenney clearly embraced the idea of supporting the Red Cross, with an annual Red Cross program, complete with entertainment, each fall. Gertie was proudly involved in coordinating this event.

Gertie spent her childhood on a farm outside of Tenney, but had many friends in town and involved herself in Tenney's town activities as a young girl. She was an intelligent child who aspired to be a schoolteacher. At the time that she graduated from the eighth grade in 1907, there was no high school in the immediate area, with Campbell High School not opening its doors as a four-year high school until 1920. So Gertie left Tenney for the Moorhead Normal School, enrolling in the two-year intermediate teacher training program. She was back in the area, at age 17, teaching in a small rural school north of Breckenridge. Like so many young female teachers of the time, she

Gertie, age 18 or 19.

was teaching kids in the eighth grade who were bigger than she was.

It was in Gertie's first year of teaching, at age 17 in 1909, that her future husband, Matthew Kapitan, moved to Tenney. In one of Gertie's horse-and-buggy rides home to Tenney, she no doubt noticed this low key, friendly new depot agent, and apparently the noticing went in both directions. Three years later, in 1920, they were married. Matt, 15 years older than Gertie, had been born in Kansas in 1877 and attended telegraph school in Wisconsin before making his way to Tenney. Gertie's marriage to Matthew Kapitan occurred in September, 1912, when she was 20 years old.

In the typical flowery language of the Breckenridge newspaper wedding accounts of the time, Gertie was called "the popular daughter of Mr. and Mrs. Reinhard, successful farmers of Tenney," and Matt was "the obliging and pleasing Soo agent at Tenney." The wedding ceremony occurred at the farm home of Gertie's parents, the Philip Reinhards, on a Wednesday evening. There was "standing room only," about 100 people. A.N. Larson, my grandfather, served as best man. The newspaper account referred to Matt and Gertie as "a most estimable couple."

Once married, the couple lived in the railroad depot, where Matt had been living as a bachelor. The family would call the depot home for many years. Photos of the Kapitan children in the 1910s and 1920s show various family poses and playtime activities on the railway platform which was, for all practical purposes, their "backyard." The family jokes that the couple's first child, Everett, was born "nine months and a day" after Matt and Gertie's wedding, and the rest of the children arrived precisely every two years, almost to the day, for the next 15 years! Gertie used to explain jokingly that she kept having more children because she needed a rest, referring to the standard eight- to nine-day bed rest that was earned after the birth of a child "so that things could go back into place." Six children were born, at home, in the depot. Matt and Gertie's eight children—seven boys and one girl—were Everett, Warren, Arnold, Gordon, Douglas, Russell, Adeline, and Lowell, who was known throughout his life as "Buck Shot". Of those eight children, all the boys have passed away, with only Adeline living today, in 2007. I had the pleasure of chatting with

82-year-old Adeline when I interviewed her in 2007. Adeline is one of the few people on the quilt who is still living. She was a delightful, intelligent woman who seemed truly joyful in reminiscing about her Tenney days.

Gertie, as the more outgoing person of the couple, was the family disciplinarian when it was needed. Matt was a gentle, soft-spoken, even-tempered man; a conscientious, steady worker who felt it important to instill a strong work ethic in his children. Word has it that Matt took only one vacation from work in his entire working life, and that was to take his son Arnold to Kansas to visit Matt's extended family. With Matt working as the depot agent for the Soo Line Railroad, the family had a railroad pass, which every so often was used by family members, but there was very little time or money for travel. Adeline recalled her first big trip away from Tenney, a visit to her Uncle Lanny's home in Edmonton, Alberta by train with her mother when she was quite young.

One can only imagine the household management skills that Gertie had to pull out of a hat in order to raise her brood and take care of her husband, church and community—all responsibilities that she took very seriously. Given the volume and intensity of her responsibilities, as well as the somewhat isolated location of little Tenney in relation to the rest of the world, Gert was somewhat insulated from the changes that were happening in the 1920s with regard to "women's work."

Nonetheless, women in Tenney may have, by 1928, heard of a "friend" named Betty Crocker, a fictional woman created by the Washburn Crosby Company of Minneapolis (later, General Mills) in 1921 to answer questions submitted by consumers about baking (Felder, 1997). In 1924, the "Betty Crocker Cooking School of the Air" debuted on NBC radio. Lots of advertising in the late 1920s featured a "caring friend" that women could write to for advice and encouragement, and Betty Crocker was an example of this trend. Between Betty Crocker and the first Miss America pageant, both created in 1921, as well as a preponderance of female motion picture starlets now accessible to the average woman, a very different standard for female beauty and identity in America was being created in the Twenties.

There was an increasing commercialization of women as attractive, sexual beings which, as shocking as it initially was, emphasized physical beauty as *the* most important characteristic a woman could have. Advertising in the Twenties encouraged women to look good for themselves but, most importantly, for others. Listerine mouth wash had a large ad campaign in the late Twenties, first "creating the problem" that women could not risk having bad breath, then referring to its mouth wash as "breath deodorant," a solution to this problem. Helena Rubenstein, Elizabeth Arden, and other beauty products came on the market, and were heavily marketed in the early Twenties, making it a $141 million industry by 1925 (Rowbotham, 1997). Rowbotham states that "American women were enthusiastically embracing consumer culture."

Advertisers of the time focused on women, recognizing that they played this important role of consumer as part of their domestic responsibilities. Consumerism had exploded in the Twenties, with women being bombarded by promises of fresher breath, beautiful hair, and absence of body odor. This set in motion a mindset in which multiple generations of women would measure their self-worth by the products they bought and the clothing, jewelry, cosmetics and beauty products that pampered or adorned their bodies. Magazines provided full-page, colorful pictures of products and women enjoying those products. Women were constantly inundated with advice regarding the virtues of cleanliness and personal hygiene.

But the consumer culture pushed products that extended well beyond the personal items that women could apparently not live without. Technological advances made housework easier; though many of these conveniences hit the Tenney scene quite a bit later than in the metropolitan areas. The advent of electric lights alone brought housework to an entirely different level. Electrification occurred in Tenney, thanks to the Ottertail Power Company, in 1914. When my great grandfather, John Polifka, and his young family returned from their three-year attempt at homesteading a plot of land near Lemon, South Dakota from 1908 to 1911, they lived for a short time on the Nadeau farm between Tenney and Campbell. Electricity was being installed in Campbell at the time. The Polifka family—John and Helen and their four children, one of whom would one day be my grandmother—stood outside in the farm yard gazing at nearby Campbell as the big switch was pulled that evening, and the magic moment occurred. That magic moment paved the way for irons, toasters, electric sewing machines, refrigerators, washing machines, and percolators to become a way of life for the housewives of Tenney and Campbell. But let's not get ahead of ourselves. Electrification did not mean that every home in Tenney had electricity. In fact, very few did initially. It took until several years later for that to occur.

It is also difficult to imagine that Gertie and others of this era managed their households without the benefit of running water. The home in which Gertie and Matt lived was finally serviced with running water in 1968, long after Matt had died and Gertie had moved out. Al and Lou Ida Manthie were living in the home when this big event happened. I learned of this big event when looking through a scrapbook of Al Manthie's, now the possession of Al's granddaughter, Sherry Swan. The arrival of water to their home was an event worthy of a photo spread in the family scrapbook and much fanfare. It is hard for little ol' suburban-raised me to imagine that Al and Lou Ida were just getting water when I was, at age 12, living in relative luxury in my home without a clue that people actually lived without flushable toilets and water faucets.

I recall visiting Great Grandma Helen Polifka in Tenney as a young child and being quite enthralled with the concept of using an outhouse. I was equally or even more enthralled with the large white enamelware object which Grandma referred to as the chamber pot—new terminology for me at the time—sitting in all its glory on the upstairs landing at the top of the stairs in her home. I kept thinking, "What if it spilled?" Rumor has it that Grandma Helen had one of the best outhouses in town, but I'm not sure of the criteria for such a judgment. I do seem to remember that there were two holes, and perhaps that's what put it at the top of the heap, so to speak. Or perhaps it was the magazine pages that wallpapered the interior of the outhouse, providing lots of visual images, as well as miscellaneous reading material, while sitting on the pot. It could have been the best outhouse, and it could have been the worst outhouse, as far as I was concerned, because it was the only one I had ever set my backside on at that point in my life. A discussion with Elaine Manthie (now Streyffeler) revealed that the Manthie family outhouse, with its two-tone sky blue and beige interior paint job, certainly would seem to rank it right up there with the best of them. Reports are that, for Tenney's annual Memorial Day reunion picnic, when upwards off 200 people would be in town in the peak reunion years, various residents would have to spruce up their outhouses in order to supplement the facilities available in the church's social hall. There are still, in 2007, many residential lots in Tenney that did not, in their entire existence as residences, have water service and, of course, now they never will.

Chances are there were very few electric refrigerators in Tenney in 1928, as they were mostly considered luxury items until the 1930s in the country as a whole (Sivulka, 1998). Most homes at that point had some sort of non-electrical ice box, and homemakers found other ingenious ways of storing food as well. Meat was often smoked or canned. And of course many homes had underground cellars, usually accessible only by a diagonally-installed door, mounted outside, near the foundation of the house, with steps or a ladder leading downward under the house. Ice was brought to Tenney by rail and stored in an ice house across the road from the railroad tracks, near the hotel. Sivulka states that, in 1925, Frigidaire sold an electric cooling system to upgrade an icebox, and the term "Frigidaire" soon became the generic term for refrigerator. How many of us can remember our grandmothers or great grandmothers referring to the refrigerator as the "Frigidaire?" General Electric followed in 1927 with its own refrigerator, the "Monitor Top," which had a cooling system on top of the refrigerator.

Americans were encouraged to buy these large ticket items—radios, automobiles, electric refrigerators—on the installment plan, the same items used by the "upper crust." Americans bought into this concept that buying such luxuries would improve their standard of living (Kirocofe, 1993). This mindset was brought about by the rapid changes in the country's economy, in which more and more goods were being produced for the consumer market. In 1928, the Ford factory was turning out literally thousands of Model As each week (Dumenil,

1995).

Automobile ownership was slower to spread among the general population of Wilkin County than in some parts of the country, but by the mid to late Twenties, automobiles were commonplace on Tenney's streets. The first car in Tenney was owned by Billy Austin, one of the early saloon keepers. Thomas B. Waite, a farmer who lived west of town and was known for expressing his opinion on a variety of topics whenever he darn well felt like it, referred to it as "Billy Austin's damned red go-devil" (Schwinn, 1984). A Mr. Finlayson had the distinction, before Billy Austin, of owning the first automobile in the county. Originally from the little Wilkin County village of Kent, Mr. Finlayson eventually moved to Breckenridge, where he owned a livery, then the first car dealership in town, selling Oaklands and Pontiacs. Since people came from all around to buy cars in Breckenridge, chances are that some of the earlier automobile owners in Tenney purchased them from Mr. Finlayson, but there were also other options. Several Tenney folks purchased new automobiles in 1928. In January, Mr. Powell drove over from White Rock (South Dakota, just 15 miles from Tenney) to park his new Ford on Tenney's Main Street so that the locals could admire it. Apparently it drew a sizable crowd of admirers by Tenney standards. In February, Walter Gore traded in his old Ford touring car at the dealership in Wheaton for a newer model. Percy Scott was cruising the streets of Tenney in a new Whippet Sport Model Runabout in June, and Hannah Dalgarno and her children were enjoying a new Ford coach in August. In November, Mr. and Mrs. Arneson of Tenney had purchased a new car from Neisess, Reyelts and Company in Campbell. Advertisements in the Breckenridge newspaper over the course of the year showed massive marketing efforts by the area car dealers. Buicks were being sold for $1,195 at Lillegard Buick Sales in Wahpeton, and Knight Sales Company in Breckenridge had several new Whippets on display. Ads also touted the new Dodge Victory Six, just on the market the summer of that year. My grandfather, who had an appreciation for shiny new automobiles, always worked in a visit to the auto show on his annual early spring buying trip to the Twin Cities.

The ***Breckenridge Gazette*** cited in December of 1928 that

6,426 motor vehicles were newly registered that year in Minnesota, making a total of 672,724 registered vehicles. By the end of the 1920s, 20% of Americans owned cars (Dumenil, 1995). In keeping with the rest of the state and indeed, the rest of the country, Tenney folks were finding that their automobiles afforded them the freedom, status and mobility that they had not previously known. Casper J. Schott, whose name appears on the quilt, had been the proprietor of a tavern and pool hall in Breckenridge since the turn of the century but in 1925, three years prior to the quilt, began an auto accessories establishment, a very up-and-coming business venture at the time.

Further illustrating the increasing interest in automobiles and automobile supplies and service was the presence of the "signature" of Firestone Tire Company on the Tenney Quilt. I am guessing that one of the business establishments in either Tenney or Campbell sold Firestone tires, or perhaps tires were sold by a salesman who was passing through. The Louie Wittman service garage, which stood immediately north of my grandfather's general store could have sold or been associated with Firestone Tires, as could the Neisses Reyelts Hardware Store and car dealership in Campbell. At any rate, someone paid a dime on behalf of the Firestone Tire Company, therefore preserving it as a piece of Tenney history.

Five other individual business names were embroidered on the quilt: Wing Ice Cream Company, which probably supplied the ice cream to Cliff's Place; Neisses Reyalts and Company, a Campbell hardware, implement, fuel, and automobile dealership; the Larson Store, which was my grandfather's general mercantile; the Grant Dady Company, which is still a mystery to me; and Kellogg Cereal Company, which has previously been described as the employer of George Engfer, who was Gertie Kapitan's brother-in-law.

Matt Kapitan's job as Soo Line agent and telegrapher provided a steady income for the Kapitan family, even though it was very modest. While farmers had their up and down years, the Kapitans felt fortunate they at least did not have to rely on the weather for their livelihood. With eight children, times were often lean for the family but with Gertie's extreme resourcefulness and thriftiness, they survived. In 1939, when Matt retired early due to his increasing hearing loss, there was a six-month gap from the time he retired until his pension checks started to come in. During this time, Matt went to my grandfather, A.N. Larson, the proprietor of the Larson General Store, and asked if A.N. would give him credit until the family received the first pension check. According to Gertie and Matt's daughter Adeline, A.N. graciously carried his good friend Matt's family to the tune of $90 in grocery bills, an astronomical amount at the time, until the family was on its feet again and could pay off their debt. Adeline has never forgotten this act of kindness by my grandfather and told me about it in great detail in 2007.

During these tough times and others, area farmers were very good to the Kapitans. Jack and Amy Richardson, whom Gert considered "best friends," were particularly generous. At butchering time, Gert let it be known that she'd take all the animal "parts" that everyone else considered waste, and would use them to feed her family. Butchering was done on the farm. Some meat was canned, some smoked and some scalded down. Sausage and head cheese was made, and lard was stored in stone jars to be used for shortening in baked goods. Blood and intestines were used for sausage [though Gertie drew the line at blood sausage, which she abhorred], and the waste fats were often used for making soap. Head cheese was a common sight on the Kapitan dinner table, and with a little resourcefulness, creativity and cooking talent, it's no telling what could be concocted from animal parts that shall heretofore remain anonymous. Lena Mann, whose signature is on the quilt, reported that she and her husband did their own butchering and made four kinds of bologna—"better than you can buy today!" (Wilkin County Historical Society, 1977).

Gertie had a large garden, and tended it with loving care in order to provide for her family and generously give to others. She canned tomatoes, made watermelon pickles, and grew cucumbers, squash, and whatever she could coax out of the ground. Gertie was a good cook, and proudly displayed, in her scrapbook, a letter from the Sanitary Food Manufacturing Company from 1933 which notifies her that she is the winner of their monthly recipe contest. Her prize winning recipe for **Lima Beans With Pork Chops** netted Gertie a ten-dollar check in the mail, a pretty decent prize for someone of Gertie's means during the Depression.

Gertie never let one thing to go waste. This thriftiness spread to all areas of her life. After her children left home, Gertie had a room in her house where the remnants of other people's yard sales were stored. Whenever things didn't sell at a garage sale, she would enthusiastically volunteer to take them off the owner's hands. And if a small piece of yarn ended up on the floor and someone tried to throw it away—Gertie would quickly remind them that it could be used as filler material for an appliquéd quilt, dish towel, or dresser scarf.

Gertie's parents, Philip and Diana Reinhard, had left Tenney in 1916 to take over the farm formerly operated by Diana's parents near Wilmot, South Dakota. They remained there the rest of their lives. After Philip's death, Diana visited Gertie's family in Tenney often, feeling very much a part of the community in which she had once been an active member. At the time Gertie and Diana's names appeared on the Tenney Quilt in 1928, Diana had lost her husband Philip four years prior, and was living with daughter Mae in Rochester, Minnesota. Diana enjoyed visiting her children and grandchildren, and spent much time with them, particularly her daughters, Gertie and Mae.

As previously mentioned, Matt and Gertie's first six children—all boys—were born in the depot's living quarters. Shortly before their daughter Adeline's birth in 1925, the Kapitans and their six boys moved into the vacant church parsonage in the absence of a resident preacher. After a brief time living in the parsonage, they purchased a home in Tenney which Gertie would occupy until she left Tenney in the early 1950s. This little square home, which stands today in 2007 in a dilapidated, unoccupied state, is located on the easternmost street in Tenney, now County Road 13, next to the home occupied for many years by Louie and Minnie Wittman (and later by their daughter Lois and husband Norris "Goog" Tracy). Barbara Holtan, Gert and Matt's granddaughter, remembers a short sidewalk along that street, which ran in front of the Kapitan house, only the length of a few lots, but long enough to provide a perfect roller skating path for Barbara and many other Kapitan children and grandchildren. When I looked at this little Kapitan house in recent years, I simply could not imagine where so many children and grandchildren could be stacked, even when one considers that, by the time they bought this house, some of the older children were off on their own in the world.

Gertie Kapitan was deeply involved in all of the women's activities in town, primarily those that were associated with the Tenney Church. Her involvement with Ladies Aid was previously mentioned. But she also served as the pianist for the Tenney Church for 40 years, and oral history indicates that, as a young girl, Gertie helped haul rocks that served as the foundation for that church, which was built entirely by volunteer community labor. One Thursday afternoon in 1930, when Gertie was 38 years old and busy raising a family, she and her friends Amy Richardson and Ann Janke decided the time had come for them to be baptized. The three women approached Reverend Miller of the Tenney Church and asked him to perform this rite, which subsequently occurred at the lake at Shady Dell Resort. The previous Sunday, two Tenney families—the Jankes and the Ilers—got caught up on baptisms, with the Ilers at the Tenney Church and the Jankes at the Taylor Church. Perhaps Gertie and her friends had been inspired by the baptisms of the younger kids earlier in the week as Doris, Vern and Myron Janke, and Francis, Anna and Lillian Iler were all baptized by Reverend Miller during the Sunday morning services at their respective churches.

Gertie is remembered by her family as someone whose hands simply never stopped. If she wasn't washing clothes, mending, or cooking, she was weeding the garden, canning vegetables, or working on any number of handwork projects such as knitting, crocheting, quilting, or making braided wool rugs. She started each January to make handmade gifts for her entire family, and worked her way through the year creating quilts, rugs, mittens, socks, embroidered towels and a multitude of other gifts for a year's worth of birthdays, Christmas gifts, and other special occasions. For a family of eight children and all their spouses and offspring, this was no small task. She would start all over again the next January, and she did this for decades. When she wasn't doing handwork, housework, or church work, Gertie loved to write letters, and she kept a diary for most of her adult life. She was an Energizer bunny.

Part of Gert's legacy was her gift of music. The Kapitan home was filled with music, always with Gert at the center playing piano and the kids singing. Many others in town were musically gifted, too. During this time period Mrs. Kuentzel gave piano lessons, and in earlier years, Mrs. McAlpin gave organ lessons. Ann Janke and others in her family were very musically talented, and Ann was usually the coordinator of anything that had to do with the church choir. Ministers' wives and school teachers were also good candidates as musical performers and leaders. Janice Anderson, grammar room teacher for the first half of 1928, was a talented singer and pianist. Russell "Red" McLaughlin was a musician of professional level talent, playing in Tenney both on his porch and at the Town Hall for many events through the years, then professionally in several honky tonk venues in the Fifties. Young Arthur Klugman and all of the Kapitan kids were musically talented. In February of 1928, the year of the quilt, a "town orchestra" was started in Tenney, with regular practices, and there were plans for numerous performances throughout the year. Whether or not those performances occurred, I cannot confirm, but during that February, anticipation and enthusiasm was running high for this musical group. Miss Anderson, teacher at the Tenney School, was the leader of this group at first violin, with Matt Kapitan at second violin. Rev. Haueter played the saxophone, Arthur Klugman, a very talented young man, played the banjo, and all were accompanied on the piano by Ann Janke. A young people's choir was also in the making that year, with plans for orchestral accompaniment. Perhaps the Tenney Orchestra was short-lived, as it lost two of its members the following spring—Miss Anderson moved on to another teaching position, and Rev. Haueter and his family left that June to serve a church in Wyoming. I can find no further references to this group in the local news column in 1928. In the Thirties, however, a 4H band formed and was active for several years.

I can't help but put my own great grandmother, Helen Polifka, at the opposite end of the musical spectrum. Maybe she could sing—I don't know—but one might question her love for her mother's organ, which sat on Grandma Helen's porch for many, many years after her mother had moved from the farm in to town. Finally, after years of exposure to the harsh elements, blowing dust, climbing grandchildren, cooling bread, and who knows what else, it was relegated to the garage in a dilapidated condition. Apparently there was not much music produced on that porch by the Polifka family. But that's not where the story ends. It appears that Grandma Helen, in her frugality, chopped up parts of the organ and used the ivories as garden markers. She saw nothing wrong with this; after all, "waste" was not a part of her vocabulary, nor that of most other women of her vintage. However, the demolition of the family organ has horrified more than one of her descendents. My mother rescued the top half of that organ many years later and had the ornately carved wooden face refinished. It now hangs on the wall of my parents' home, serving beautifully as a place to display their flow blue china collection.

Following Matt Kapitan's funeral service in 1947, the Kapitan family carried on its musical tradition by gathering around the piano and singing as their mother played the hymns they had all sung as a family through the years. For an hour and a half they filled their home with music and celebrated the life of "the obliging and pleasing Soo agent." And at the occasion of her 90th birthday celebration, Gertie

was asked if she'd like to play something for the group that had gathered. She sat down and played, in the words of her daughter Adeline, "a perfect rendition of *The Missouri Waltz,*" to the delight of her family and friends.

Gertie was the rural correspondent to both the Wheaton and the Breckenridge newspapers for several years, providing local Tenney news—commonly referred to as "The Locals"—to the newspaper readers of the time. As it turns out, it was the Kapitan children who did much of the legwork. In the 1930s, it was

Gertie

Adeline and Russell Kapitan who found the scoops on the streets of Tenney. Every Monday afternoon after the Tenney School bell rang,

Adeline and Russell divided the town of Tenney right up the middle and each claimed half. Adeline started this as a ten-year-old; Russell, was twelve. Gordon and Douglas probably had a stint in previous years, and may have been the news gatherers at the time of the Tenney quilt. Who knows—maybe the older children had their turn. Adeline reports that the kids knocked on every door in their half of the town—that would be one square block each—asking each woman of the house if she had any news to put in the paper. This part of the process, according to Adeline, took about an hour and a half. The kids took their job very seriously, making notes at each stop in which a newsworthy event had taken place during the past week.

The notes were then brought home and given to their mother, Gertie, who added this information to any other news tidbits she had been given during the week in the course of her daily networking. Gertie then, "using two fingers" as Adeline recalls, typed the report and put it in an envelope, which had to be on the Monday evening train to Breckenridge. A portion of the Kapitan family followed some version of this ritual literally every week for what I believe may have been three decades. Doris Raguse took over the correspondent duties once Gertie left town.

Here are just a few of my favorite entries in the "Tenney locals" around the Tenney Quilt years. These statements are written as they appeared in their entirety:

- "Maurice Roach has been entertaining the chicken pox since the holiday vacation."

- "Victor Kath and Pearl Iler got 100 in Spelling last week."

- "The club met last Wednesday evening at Mrs. Jerome Dawson's. They had plum pudding with lemon sauce."

- "A few of the Tenneyites attended the married folks dance at Fairmount last Friday night."

- "Mrs. George Dopp spent last Thursday canning meat."

- "Friends of Harding Parks were pleased to hear he sat at the table for Christmas dinner."

- "Percy Scott is enjoying the pleasures of a new Whippet sport model Runabout."

- "A.N. Larson went fishing at Ten Mile Lake last Friday night."

- "A few of the young folks danced at the hall last Wednesday night till midnight."

- "Clifford Polifka autoed to Breckenridge last Tuesday."

And then there is my all-time favorite:

- "Pumpkin Center was robbed of a good pipe wrench and two quarts of oil."

Any particular item is not necessarily fall-on-the-floor funny. But I must admit that these quirky little news tidbits tickle me. It is easy to joke about the newsworthiness or lack of newsworthiness—from our 21st century perspective—of the news items that appeared in the Tenney locals through the years. But all joking aside, the historical value of such documentation of this small town's life is, to me, astounding. Traditional historical accounts may document the origin of the town, the primary businesses and their contribution to the town, historical characters of significance—who tended to be men—and perhaps demographic data. But what about Tenney's human history? Who better to write about daily life in Tenney than a woman who had lived in this town her entire life, had eight children who attended the local school, served as the pianist in the local church for 40 years, was married to a man who worked at the local railroad depot, and was involved in all the women's social groups in the area? How else but through "The Locals" could one really understand the social structure of the town—the relationships—the intertwining of lives—the trends and values and influences—of a little village that otherwise is remembered only through family histories or brief mention in a local county history book? Imagine what we could learn about the place and the times if we would read the Tenney locals over a period of decades. We can laugh at the issues that Gertie and her contemporaries such as Minnie Church, the rural correspondent for neighboring

Campbell, felt were important enough to report to the readership of the **Breckenridge Gazette** or the **Wheaton Gazette**, but it is important to also recognize this as a truly legitimate means in which the women of Tenney wrote its real, true history.

Gertie was a staunch Republican. In October of 1928, the Hoover-Curtis campaign bus rolled in to Breckenridge with political speaker, Senator Pitt of Iowa, campaigning for the Hoover-Curtis Republican presidential ticket. The bus stopped in front of the Farmers and Merchants Bank in Breckenridge, with music playing to attract people to the street corner. Tenney organized a "Hoover Club" with the help of an organizer, Mrs. Gordon, from the Minneapolis Republican Headquarters, who gave a talk about "our next president." Our Gertie was elected president of Tenney's Hoover Club, with Amy Richardson as vice-president, and new school teacher Janice Johnson as secretary. On election night, several women kept vigil at the I.O.O.F. Hall in Tenney waiting for the election returns [presumably on the radio], which Gertie reported in her column as being "very gratifying and well worth sitting up for." Once the election was won, coffee and doughnuts were served to those who had sat out the evening. As it turns out, the vote was quite close in Campbell Township (of which Tenney is a part), with 91 votes for Herbert Hoover and 70 votes for Al Smith, even though Hoover won the election in a landslide nationally.

It is apparent that Jack and Rose O'Laughlin and their friends, J.J. and Theresa McIntyre of Campbell, were staunch supporters of Democratic candidate Al Smith, and even went to see him in person at an appearance in the region in early October, 1928. Accounts in later years report the O'Laughlins' attendance at political conventions. Jack O'Laughlin was the manager of the Farmers Elevator in Tenney, and J.J. McIntyre had the same position at the Farmers Elevator in Campbell. Mr. McIntyre was the mayor of Campbell several times, served on the school board, and was elected president of the Village Council the year after the Tenney Quilt. The O'Laughlins were well-respected, upstanding citizens of Tenney, reaching a place which allowed them some of the finer things in life, by Tenney standards. Their home, as previously mentioned, was the first to have running water and an indoor toilet. And in May of 1934, our Gertie reported that

"Mrs. Jack O'Laughlin is enjoying the use of a new Kelvinator" which is, of course, an electric refrigerator. However, it appeared Walter and Belle Gore get the points for having the first television in town. The O'Laughlins and McIntyres were Catholic, perhaps shedding light on their support of the Catholic Democratic candidate, Al Smith, a fact that may interfere with our 21st century political correctness, but which was quite common in that era. I have to believe that Hoover Club President Gertie felt just a little bit smug when her candidate Hoover defeated Al Smith in the presidential election, given that the O'Laughlins and McIntyres were considered the "upper crust" of Tenney and Campbell at the time.

Matt died in 1947 at the age of 70, after eight years of retirement. Tenney's population had experienced a slow and steady decline. The school was in its last days of operation (closing finally in 1956); young people had grown up, moved away, and not returned; and businesses were closing as their proprietors retired or passed away. Gertie, at age 55, would have nothing to do with easing into a life of relaxation and retirement, and still had a lot of mothering left in her. As difficult as I believe it was for Gert to close the door of her little square house one last time and say good-bye to the town where she had lived her entire adult life up to that point, Gertie thought it was perhaps time to move on. She found employment as a house mother at the Morris Ag School.

Initially built as a Native American boarding school, the West Central School of Agriculture had been established in Morris in 1910, and served as an area high school with a boarding school environment (Regents of Univ of MN, 2006). It operated as a high school until 1963. My mother and her friend from Tenney, Ruth Ann Ahlstein, attended this high school, graduating in 1950.

During the school year, Gertie lived in a dormitory building, serving as the away-from-home mother that many of these young high school girls needed, as it was most often their first experience living away from home for an extended period of time. Being a one-time teacher and a well-practiced mother, this job as house mother fit Gertie to a tee. She filled her summers between school years by working as a cook at a resort near Brainerd, Minnesota, another job that suited her well because, after all, cooking and mothering were the things that Gertie knew best. After her stint at Morris, Gertie then lived with her daughter Adeline for a short period of time before moving to an apartment in Breckenridge. She continued to live in Breckenridge for about ten years, retaining many of her friendships from Tenney, particularly that of Amy Richardson, who had been her best friend for most of her life and for decades, had popped her head in to Gertie's back door, and said, "YOO HOO!"

A turning point in Gertie's life came in 1975, when Gertie was 83 years old. It was that year that her son, Arnold, died suddenly of a heart attack at age 58. Gertie was a strong, faithful woman and always had been so, but according to her daughter Adeline, Gertie was overcome with grief for her son and for this event that hadn't occurred in life's natural order. Arnold's death was followed two years later by the death of Gertie's dear friend, Amy. It was a tough time in Gertie's life.

It became evident, at age 90, that Gertie could not live as independently as she once had. She moved to an apartment at a senior complex in the Twin Cities to be closer to several of her children and grandchildren. She loved living in the apartment and true to form, made many friendships and found meaningful things to keep her hands busy. However, being later moved to the nursing home section of that facility after a series of strokes was very sad for Gertie, who had vowed she would never live in such a place, and had asked her children not to let that happen. Her daughter Adeline counts it among the saddest days of her own life when, on the first day of Gertie's stay in the nursing home, her mother said to her, "I don't understand where I am or why I am here." They had moved Gertie to her nursing home room before Adeline was able to arrive and help Gertie through this transition.

Gertie lived only two and a half months after that day. She died in 1985 after living a long and happy life of 93 years. A town has "forefathers" and a town has "foremothers." Gertie Kapitan is truly a "foremother" of Tenney, playing an integral part in the lives of so many of its people. Every person who lived in Tenney during Gertie's lifetime had heard her piano playing, read her news accounts in the

Breckenridge or Wheaton newspaper, sampled her baked goods at pie socials at the town hall, tasted her homemade pickles, and greeted her on the sidewalks of Tenney. Gertie raised eight children who, at a time when it was not the norm, all graduated from high school and in many cases, from college. Like all the other women of Tenney, Gertie never did anything famous. But she darned socks, carried in wood and water, stocked cellar shelves with pickles, raised a family, and took care of her friends, her church and her community. That is her legacy.

CHAPTER 5

- The Nurses -

Violet

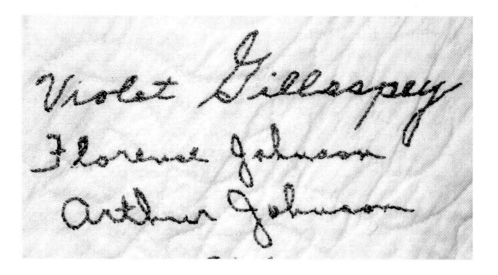

In 1928, 18-year-old Violet Gillaspey was teetering on the brink of adulthood, beginning a journey that would lead her far away from the streets of tiny Tenney to the Deep South. Violet had been born in 1910 to Charlie and Lillian Belle Herron Gillaspey, one of five children. She had three brothers, Lester, Marvin and Donald, and a younger sister, Grace. In 1928, the family was farming in the Tenney area. Violet's grandfather, 71-year-old Cicero Gillaspey, was also living with the family on the farm.

Anyone who ever lived in Tenney remembers "Pumpkin Center," a gas station and garage, with caretaker's home, that stood at a crossroads two miles straight west of Tenney. Pumpkin Center, where my

mother would later go for pre-teen slumber parties at the home of her
friend, Darlene Thiel, was opened in the year of our quilt, 1928, by
bulk oil driver Bob Neuman of Wheaton. My great great uncle, Frank
Polifka, was hired to manage the place. Bob had moved the office portion of the old Salzer Lumber Company of Tenney to this crossroads
to become the garage at Pumpkin Center. Today, any evidence that
Pumpkin Center even existed is long gone. A nondescript crossing of
two roads, with sugar beet fields on all four corners instead marks the
spot.

An old abandoned farmhouse and barn stood about two miles west
of Pumpkin Center that was known through the Forties and Fifties as
"the Gillaspey place," so this was most likely where Violet Gillaspey's
family lived. In fact Mr. Gillaspey served as the proprietor of Pumpkin
Center in the early 1930s. Violet Gillaspey's future daughter Gloria,
who never lived on that farm, went back to visit "the Gillaspey place"
in later years, and remembers it as having many apple trees.

Violet would have attended either the Tenney School, or perhaps
what was known as the "Little Red School," from Kindergarten through
the 8th grade. Most Tenney kids who continued their education to the
high school level often did so in Campbell or Tintah, only a few miles
away. However, several young people spread out to other high schools
in western Minnesota locales such as Breckenridge, Morris, Wheaton,
or Elbow Lake. Often a student's choice of high school was determined
by the location of grandparents or other relatives who could provide
free, or at least minimal, room and board. Violet attended high school
in Elbow Lake, Minnesota, one of four young Tenney kids who did so
in 1928. The other three were my uncles, Ralph and Andrew Larson,
and Warren Kapitan, son of Matt and Gertie Kapitan. I don't know exactly where Violet boarded during her Elbow Lake High School years
or what determined her decision to attend high school there. At any
rate, she graduated in 1928.

In late summer of 1928, the exact time that signatures were being collected for the Tenney Quilt, a surprise going-away party was
being planned for Violet at her home, in anticipation of her departure
for St. Paul to begin nurse's training at Ancker Hospital. Violet was
embarking, with her friend Pauline Glud, on what must have seemed

at the time to be an adventure of grand proportions. St. Paul was a pretty fair distance from Tenney—about 170 miles—at least in the eyes of many who lived in Tenney. However, it seemed as though the Tenney kids who boarded in other towns for high school were the least intimidated by a potential move to "the big city" for further education or work. After all, by being away from their parents and immediate family while at high school, they had already gotten a taste of independence, even if only during the week. Pauline Glud and her younger brother, originally from Washington State, were living in Tenney at the time with her aunt and uncle, Susan and John Johnson. The Johnsons, farmers of Norwegian ancestry, had been raising Pauline and her younger brother for at least the previous eight years. Sending one's children off to live with relatives was not necessarily uncommon in those days, when life expectancies were short, accidental deaths were commonplace, and reliance on extended family was much stronger.

The activities of the young people in town in 1928, when Violet was 18 years old, were plentiful. No different than today, groups of young people often gathered at the home of one of the other kids. They played cards, often *Rook* or *500*, until late in the evening, when the mother of the house would make a midnight snack or even a meal for the group. There was a very active group of young teens and young-20s in Tenney at this time who had very little trouble finding things to do, either inside or outside.

"Going to the lake" is just part of life for those of us who live in central and northern Minnesota, and it was part of the life for Tenney folks, too. If you lived in Tenney, there was really only one place to conveniently "go to the lake," but it was quite a popular destination. That was Ten Mile Lake, about twenty miles northeast of town. All the end-of-school-year picnics were held at Ten Mile Lake with entire families enjoying food, games, swimming, and fishing. Just about any social, church, or community group held picnics and outings at Ten Mile Lake at one point or another. It was also commonplace for a Tenney family to pack up a picnic and go to Ten Mile Lake on Sunday afternoon after church. My grandfather was known to do so, both to pursue his love of fishing and to escape the inevitable Sunday emergency requests to open the Larson Store for a can of beans.

Violet had close friends in Dorothy Klugman and Elaine Ready, though they were younger. Still in high school, Dorothy and Elaine attended Wheaton High School while living with their grandparents. But it was back to Tenney on the weekends and in the summertime. Violet and Dorothy made frequent jaunts to Elaine's farm home on Friday evenings. Imagine sending your teenage daughter off into the country on a dark Friday night on foot for a three- to four-mile hike, accompanied by an equally young female friend. In 1928, it was simply the only sure way for two young teenage girls to get around. As it would turn out, Elaine followed in her friend Violet's footsteps and began her own nurses' training only a few years later at St. Francis Hospital School of Nursing in Breckenridge.

Smoking, drinking and cosmetics, traditionally associated with prostitutes before that time, became accessible to the young women of the Twenties, no doubt creating a bit of a buzz in Tenney. I am quite sure that Elizabeth Parks and Belle Gore just about flipped their lids when they were first exposed to the cigarette-smoking, Charleston-dancing, gin-drinking, scantily clad, suntanned women known as "flappers." Cigarettes were sold during the Twenties, but smoking was still very controversial for women throughout the decade. In Tenney or elsewhere in the rural Midwest, the sight of a woman with a Camel, Lucky Strike or Chesterfield would have at the very least, raised eyebrows, and more likely, caused one to think such a woman was a bit crass and—well—"loose."

The cover of the August, 1928, *American Girl* magazine shows a young woman playing tennis in a knee-length white dress—a very modern image at the time. A *Vogue* magazine cover in the same year shows a svelte woman, perfectly coiffed with a permanent wave, wearing a bright yellow knee-length business suit with a tunic-style top. She is standing on the roof of a building in a mid-stride pose, with a large city skyline serving as the backdrop. Looking confidently into her compact mirror, she is no doubt admiring the face which had been made up with a variety of cosmetic products. Media images even showed women lighting up a Lucky Strike. School girls, teenagers, young women, and housewives began to be bombarded in magazines, movies, and radio by women who expressed their individualism and questioned traditional values and morals. While these images represented concepts and practices that took much longer to reach the rural Midwest, the young women in Tenney still had access to these images and thus, began to expand their own ideas about modern women.

While women's magazines touted the new American woman, it was clear that the conservative stalwarts of American printed media such as *Time* magazine, had a bit of trouble turning the equity corner. Each issue of *Time* in 1928 featured a full-head photograph of a person of national interest. The only three women to grace the cover of *Time* during the entire year of 1928 were Ruth Hanna McCormick, the publisher and president of the Rockford Consolidated Newspaper in Rockford, Illinois; Maria Jeritza, a Czech opera soprano who sang at the Metropolitan Opera in New York City in Puccini's "Tosca"; and First Lady Grace Goodhue Coolidge (Rowbotham, 1997).

A new, less inhibited dancing style became popular during the Twenties. For the young women, their dancing was symbolic of the rejection of the traditionally accepted appearance and style of behavior—really no different, I suppose, than today's "hip hop" or any number of other modern dances that the previous generation looks at and scratches their collective head. These women of the Twenties were newly independent, seeking new ways of self-expression, and the young Tenney women were no exception, even though Tenney probably brought up the rear in terms of fashion and pop culture trends. The Town Hall's dance floor was the site of many dances, normally on Friday nights, where the "Shimmy Shake," the "Black Bottom," and the "Lindy Hop" replaced the waltz and fox trot for the younger generation. When the young people of Tenney wished to shimmy and shake outside the watchful glances of Tenney's elders, Fairmount, just seven miles west and the next town on the Soo Line Railroad, was a popular option in the Twenties. Dancing, for the strictest of Christians—yes, even for some German Americans—was frowned upon, and Elaine Manthie remembers hearing stories of the local minister peering out the window of his second-floor bedroom in the parsonage across the street from the Town Hall, perhaps making a mental note of the dance patrons entering its doors. Jennie Waite, Mrs. Hiatt, and Helen Polifka often served midnight lunches for the crowd at the Town Hall. Usually it was sandwiches, pickles, cake and coffee, which the patrons paid 50 cents per couple and ate at tables set up in the Town Halls' balcony (Schwinn, 1984). With no café in town, it was up to the Tenney women to provide this service during or after dances and special events. After the midnight lunch, there would be even more dancing, afterwards, until 1:00 or 1:30 a.m.

Lawrence Welk and his contemporaries provided as much excitement as the older generation cared to experience. During the late 1920s Welk, just in his twenties at the time, was doing one-nighters across the Midwest with his bands, "Lawrence Welk and His Hotsy Totsy Boys," and later, "Lawrence Welk and His Honolulu Fruit Gum Orchestra." Rumor has it that The Hotsy Totsy Boys played in the Tenney Town Hall at some point in the late Twenties, though it would not have necessarily been a big deal at the time since Lawrence Welk was just another band leader at that point. In the Thirties, Welk's band expanded its tour area, leaving the small-time venues such as the Tenney Town Hall, in its dust. German old-time music was also popular in the area, particularly since New Ulm's Whoopee John Wilfahrt had begun regular broadcasts on Twin Cities radio in 1924 (Conzen, 2003).

There was no shortage of outdoor recreation in Tenney in the Twenties. The town had its own lighted tennis and horseshoe court and on some weekend days it was busy from dawn to dusk. Late in the year of 1928, a fence was even built around the court. Young people would head out to someone's country home for a wiener roast, and in the winter, they made their own homemade ice cream and licked the dasher. The town basketball team played against neighboring teams such as Tintah, Barrett and Doran, in the Town Hall. The Pithey pasture, just south of town across the railroad tracks, had been converted into a baseball field and early in Tenney's history, a half-mile race track for horse races.

My great grandfather, John Peter Polifka, played catcher on the Tenney baseball team at the turn of the century. Old Johnny is credited for thinking up the "10E" logo that appeared on the front of the jerseys the team wore while competing on their field of dreams. Gertie Kapitan's father, Phil Reinhard, played first base and didn't wear a mitt. Whether that was an intentional demonstration of testosterone-induced macho behavior or an economic necessity, we will never know. Jack Richardson, known as one of the better athletes on the team, pitched for the team, and also played for Campbell and Fairmount at various points in his life. Tenney's love of baseball continued through the years and in 1928, was still an activity that provided spectating opportunities for the young and old of Tenney. It was clearly a popular pastime in the entire region at that time, as Breckenridge had what was considered a top quality baseball park, with bleachers to sit 700 people. Amateur teams from all over the country had Breckenridge on their circuit, and newspaper accounts from the era report literally thousands of fans turning out to see these teams play ball.

Kitten ball games were frequent in the Garske pasture, as well as in the school yard. Roller skating was popular, both on the town's sidewalks and on the Town Hall floor. In the Thirties, a gentleman made the circuit to many of the dance halls in western Minnesota with a box full of strap-on roller skates. Tenney was one of his regular stops, as was the town hall in Nashua, just up the road a piece. On a weekly basis, kids of all ages would come running, pay a few cents, and skate the night away at the Town Hall. Later on, Al Manthie, who served as the Village Clerk and as such, was the "keeper" of the Town Hall, purchased the skates and stored them in the Town Hall so that kids could roller skate more frequently.

Many young people hiked or hitched rides to neighboring towns such as Wahpeton or Fairmount, North Dakota or Tintah on summer nights to watch a moving picture, which was projected outside on a building or bed sheet. Although some movies released in 1928 had sound, most were still silent. Big time films in the larger metropolitan areas that year were *The Singing Fool* (a musical/drama starring Al Jolson), *Lights of New York* (a crime/drama starring Helene Costello and Cullen Landis), and *West of Zanzibar* (a horror/drama starring Lon Chaney and Lionel Barrymore) (Wikimedia Foundation, 2007). Disney's *Steamboat Willie* also premiered in 1928, the first film to include a soundtrack completely created after filming.

Hunting, trapping, and fishing were very popular for the young men of the Tenney area in 1928. There was an abundance of game, waterfowl, prairie chickens, and fox in Wilkin County, with no limits in the early years. Though initially pursued as an economic necessity, these outdoor activities showed, in 1928, the beginnings of the frenzy that now surrounds the sports of hunting and fishing in Minnesota. Max Brown, whose signature appears on the quilt along with his wife, Bertha, raised Irish Wolfhounds, which they trained for fox hunting, and shipped all over the country. Marvin Gillaspey, at age 19 in 1928, camped out at his friend Harold Scott's farm more than once that year, where they spent much time trapping muskrat around Mud Lake, east of Tenney. The Larson boys loved to hunt duck and pheasant, and were avid fishermen like their father. In 1928, Wilkin County offered a 10-cent bounty on crows, providing some pocket change for enterprising boys and men (Kron, 1937). There were also bounties on wolves and other critters deemed to be nuisances. So it seems that Violet and her young Tenney friends found ways to socialize and adequately entertain themselves without the benefit of computers, cable TV, video games, and i-Pods.

One person that seemed to take exception to the idea that there was plenty to do in Tenney was the Mexican señorita that Leland Roach brought back from one of his annual middle age jaunts to Mexico and made his wife later on in Tenney's history. It seems that the young lady stayed long enough in Tenney to marry Leland and have a child, but left shortly thereafter, explaining that living in Tenney was like living in a cemetery for the lack of activity.

Unfortunately, some folks in the area, whether natives or drifters on their way through, sought recreation of the wayward type during the late Twenties, as evidenced in the local news reports sent to the Breckenridge newspaper. Livestock was a common target. Gertie Kapitan reported that B.T. Cross, a very successful local farmer, had several pigs stolen, and Mrs. Stelton had most of her poultry taken, though the thieves did leave a few ornery hens behind. Chicken thievery was apparently quite common around Tenney and presumably in the general area. The newspaper reported, also, that the Roaches had all their fall crop of apples stolen off their trees. I suppose it is impolite to find humor from someone else's misfortune, but my very favorite news item from the quilt era was reported by Gertie, in its entirety, to the **Breckenridge Gazette** in these words: "Pumpkin Center was robbed of a good pipe wrench and two quarts of oil."

Tenney dealt with its perpetrators by throwing them in the town jail, a room in the back of the 14 x 26-foot fire hall, a quaint building that is currently listed on the National Register of Historical Places. However, this designation apparently does not carry with it the obligation to keep up the building or maintain its integrity as it stands, unfortunately, in a similar dilapidated state as most other Tenney buildings.

All of these activities—all except the thievery, I suppose—point to the availability of entertainment for Violet Gillaspey and her contemporaries. Most people who grew up in Tenney in the early days will tell you that there was never a shortage of things to do to keep busy. During this September, 1928, time period there were several references to social events and get-togethers surrounding the impending departure of Violet Gillaspey to nursing school.

The St. Francis School of Nursing had been established in 1908, just up the road from Tenney, in Breckenridge, and in the fall of 1928 had opened its doors to eleven new student nurses. At the time, it was a two-year program. Though Violet did not attend this nursing school, its course list gives us an inkling of the course work that Violet would most likely have in store for her at the Ancker Hospital School of Nursing:

- Ethics and Chemistry

- Operating Room Technique

- Drugs and Solutions

- Bacteriology

- History of Nursing

- Hygiene

- Anatomy and Physiology

- Practical Nursing

- Obstetrics

- Guinecology (spelled this way)

- Professional Topics

Dr. Wray, whose name appears on the Tenney Quilt, practiced medicine in Campbell, Tenney's closest neighboring town. He lectured to these St. Francis nursing students every Tuesday evening on the subject of neuro-psychiatry. Dr. Wray had come to Campbell in 1912 and by the time he retired in 1956, had served Campbell, Tenney, and the surrounding area for 44 years and had delivered 6,000+ babies (Erickson, 1971).

In July 1928, as Violet Gillaspey and Pauline Glud were soon to be starting their nurses' training at Ancker Hospital, another young lady from Tenney, Carrie Raguse, was finishing up her nurses' training at the same hospital and would soon be working as a nurse in Graceville, Minnesota. Perhaps it was Carrie who influenced Violet to attend nursing school at Ancker Hospital, as opposed to the closer option of St. Francis Nursing School. Violet did not know that, only two months into her nursing education in the fall of 1928, one of the most significant discoveries in medicine, the invention of penicillin, would forever change the way doctors and nurses treated illnesses.

Why Violet chose Ancker Hospital, we will never know, but its School of Nursing certainly had a good reputation, and the hospital itself would one day become one of the most respected trauma centers in the nation. The Ancker Hospital School of Nursing started in 1871, and graduated student nurses through 1976 (Health Partners Inc., 2004). The hospital has become today what is known as Regions Hospital, St. Paul's primary trauma center and hospital of great renown, particularly known for its Burn Center. The hospital started as "City and County Hospital," then went through several name changes including Ancker Hospital, St. Paul-Ramsey Hospital, and St. Paul-Ramsey Medical Center. In 1913, just 15 years before Violet set off to begin her nursing education, Ancker was the 10th largest hospital in the country, and the largest west of Chicago (Health Partners Inc., 2004).

The life of a nursing student and afterwards, as a hospital nurse, was not a walk in the park. A brochure describing the life of a nurse at the Swedish Hospital School of Nursing in Minneapolis sheds light on the working conditions for a nurse during that time: *"All nurses are required to be sober, honest, truthful, punctual, quiet, orderly, cleanly, neat, patient, kind, cheerful, and obedient to rules. Hours of duty, day nurses 7 A.M. to 7 P.M.; night nurses 7 P.M. to 7:30 A.M. Leisure hours, when possible one hour every day; one afternoon a week, and half of Sundays."* (Bingham, 1989)

In 1928, Violet's brother Lester was serving on the U.S.S. Rochester near Nicaragua. A sequence of events reported in the newspaper throughout the year of 1928 told tales of Lester's adventures. In early January, it was reported he had won several medals in target shooting and that the ship had recently moved from Balboa to Corinto. In July, it was reported that Lester had recently completed a radio devices course and was still aboard the U.S.S. Rochester. In September, Lester's parents received a note indicating that Lester had been wounded in the foot and had been in the hospital for a month. They had been worried about his safety, having heard nothing from him for quite some time. All of these events would have been happening about the time that Violet was preparing to leave home to attend nursing school.

One year later, Violet, having been home in Tenney for a period of time, was expected to leave in early August for Fergus Falls, where she would be employed at the Fergus Falls State Hospital there. The Ancker Hospital nursing program was a three-year program, and Violet would only have been a student there, at this point, for one year. So she apparently just completed a one-year practical nurse program and not a full registered nurse program. Or perhaps she was continuing her education at Fergus Falls, as Violet is referred to in local newspaper accounts as a "student nurse at Fergus Falls" on numerous occasions as late as 1930. At any rate, it appeared that Violet chose not to stay in St. Paul and instead, come back to the home territory. Perhaps, like Nellie Dalgarno, she determined that big city life was just not her thing. She lived in the nurses' living quarters right on campus at Fergus Falls. On several occasions, her parents went to Fergus Falls to pick her up on a Friday evening, brought her home to

Tenney, and delivered her back on Sunday afternoon. The two-week vacations she was awarded each year for working there were spent at home in Tenney visiting family. Census records show that Violet was still employed, in 1930, as a 19-year-old nurse at the "Fergus Falls State Hospital for the Insane."

The State Hospital for the Insane in Fergus Falls, as it was known during this time period, has a significant connection to the Tenney Quilt. It appears that our Miss Violet Gillaspey holds the key to an entire block of names on the quilt. Census records indicate that 12 of these names on one quilt square belonged to young women who, at least during the 1930 census, were employed as nurses at the Fergus Falls State Hospital for the Insane, and would have worked there at the same time as Violet Gillaspey.

The term "nurse" was used in 1928 for positions ranging from what we now know as nursing assistants, to practical nurses, to registered nurses, as well as student nurses. These young women all lived in nurses' quarters on the grounds of the hospital, and ranged in age from 16 to 28. These are the young Fergus Falls nurses whose names appear on the Tenney Quilt in addition to Violet Gillaspey:

- Lorna Griffin, age 16

- Ruth Griffin, age 17

- Helen Heald, age 16

- Helen Hoban, age 16

- Florence Johnson, age 17

- Agnes Propp, age 18

- Clara Rice, age 18

- Idella Sarmen, age 23

- Lena Sletvold, age 28

- Fay Sloan, age 18

- May Sloan, age 17

- Zelta Marie Whitaker, age 22

What a delightful surprise when I was able to connect these names to the state hospital and to our Tenney girl, Violet Gillaspey. The hospital, at this time, was only 25 years old, having originally been built to alleviate overcrowding at the Minnesota State Hospital for the Insane in St. Peter and the Rochester Asylum for Inebriates. Until 1969, the facility was a self-contained community with a 637-acre farm that included orchards, a pasture, dairy and horse barns, 35 acres of gardens, and 650 tillable acres (Hurley, 2004). The facility held, at times, up to 2,000 patients.

Yet another Tenney connection exists with the Fergus Falls State Hospital, in the person of Florence Doleman, who also worked there as a nurse. She met her future husband, Dr. Nathan Doleman, while employed at the hospital, and they eventually lived in Campbell, where "Doc" Doleman practiced for many years. Their daughter, Grace, eventually married my great uncle, Clifford Polifka, the owner of the pool hall and tavern in Tenney. After Doc Doleman's death, Mrs. Doleman moved to Tenney herself.

Our Miss Violet Gillaspey had been working at what eventually became the Fergus Falls State Hospital for three years when a young man from Indiana, traveling for Texaco Oil Company, had occasion to travel to Minnesota, and somehow crossed paths with Violet. Lewis Clyde Clemmens had been born in 1895 in Kentucky and moved to Kokomo, Indiana, with his family at age three. I do not know the details of Violet and Lewis' courtship, but things progressed, and they were married. Gertie Kapitan, who reported that Lewis and Violet were married in Texas, had a great deal of fondness for Violet and wrote in her column, "All learned to know and highly respect Violet and wish her and her husband a happy and prosperous and long married life."

Until conversing with Violet's daughter, Gloria, I could not put the pieces of Violet's life together once she left the Fergus Falls State Hospital, and they're still a bit fuzzy in places. The couple married in 1934, and their first child, Gloria Mae, was born in Nebraska that same year. How they landed in Nebraska, I am not certain, but presumably Lewis had left his job with Texaco and by that time, was working as a painter. The family did not have an easy time making ends meet, and moved frequently in order for Mr. Gillaspey to find work.

Seven years later, I picked up the family again, as Lewis registered for the World War II draft at age 46. He and Violet were living, at the time, in Eudora, Arkansas. In addition to painting, he apparently raised chickens, as his occupation was listed as "poultry" on his draft registration. Their daughter Gloria does remember that there were often chickens wherever they lived. At the time that Lewis signed up to serve his country in 1941, Lewis and Violet had a large family, with seven children born in a span of 16 years from 1934 to 1950. With the family's frequent moves, the children were born in several different states.

From Arkansas, Lewis and Violet moved at some point to Poydras Parish, New Orleans, in an area called "New Roads," where they spent the rest of their lives. Lewis died in 1964 in New Roads and is buried, as a veteran, at Alexandria National Cemetery in Pineville, Louisiana.

After Lewis' death, Violet moved into "the projects" in New Orleans, originally inhabited by lower and middle class whites and immigrants. I have often wondered if those buildings were destroyed in Hurricane Katrina. Violet's daughter indicated that, in the early 1970s, Violet's family was no longer comfortable with the increasing influx of African Americans and a skyrocketing crime rate in the projects, so they moved their mother to an apartment in a different part of town, where she died a few years later, in 1978. She is also buried at the Alexandria National Cemetery.

I enjoyed a conversation with Violet's daughter, Gloria, in 2006, who indicated most of her childhood was spent in Louisiana. Gloria reported that at the time of our conversation in 2006, four of Lewis and Violet's children were still living: three daughters (Gloria, Joyce and Glenny Lea) and one son, Gerry, who she presumes is living but who has not remained in contact with the family.

At the time Violet signed her name on the Tenney Quilt, she was 18 years old, just beginning a long journey that would bring her far from the tiny village of Tenney, to the Deep South. Like so many young women of the time, she pursued her career only up until the time she was married. At that point she was expected to stay at home and take care of her husband, the children, and household needs. Violet, according to her daughter, never worked again outside the home as a nurse. Violet's name appears on the quilt along with her mother, Lillian, her father, Charles, and her brother, Lester.

Bertha

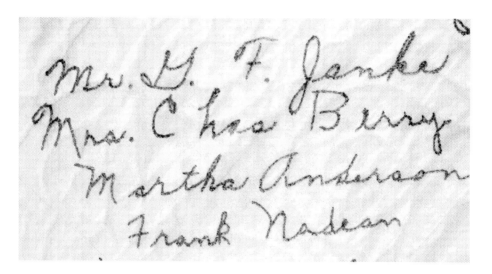

Bertha Berry was not born and raised in Tenney, nor did she work in Tenney. But Bertha's signature appears on the quilt, and her life story is intertwined with Tenney's. In 1928, Bertha would have been age 51. She had had career aspirations as a nurse for quite some time, but went about it in an entirely different way than our Miss Violet, in that Bertha started her career *after* raising her family, at age 47, four years prior to the Tenney Quilt.

Bertha Elizabeth Wikoff was born in 1876 in Ohio, a descendent of French traders who came to the Ohio Territory in the late 1600s. When Bertha was age 21 (in 1897), her family moved to Chandler, Oklahoma Territory to try cotton farming. They grew cotton on the Deep Fork Bottoms, east of Chandler. Bertha, described by a cousin as "a vivacious redhead," became an expert cotton picker (Nickel, 1984).

While in Oklahoma, Bertha met Charles Berry, a sawyer originally from Colorado. At age 24, Bertha married Charlie, in 1900. Three daughters were born to them while in Oklahoma, Mary Belle, Elva Mae and Grace Juanita.

In 1910, when most of the saw timber was gone in Oklahoma, Charles and Bertha gathered their three young daughters and moved to Ekalaka, Montana, lured by reports of enough timber to support them for many years. Two more daughters, Ethel and Luella, were born in Montana. Bertha spent the next 14 years raising her daughters and enjoying an active life in Ekalaka. At age 47, as her children were growing up and required less direct care, Bertha decided to formalize her education and obtain a nursing credential. However, living far from any school which could provide her with such a credential, Bertha decided that the U.S. Postal Service held the key. She began a correspondence course in Nursing from the Chautauqua School of Nursing during the summer of 1924.

The Chautauqua School of Nursing opened in Jamestown, New York in 1902 as a correspondence school in nursing, chartered by New York State (source: Stephen Greenberg, National Library of Medicine, the National Institutes of Health). I am not sure of the exact structure as it would have existed in 1924 when Bertha took the course but in 1918, students at the school paid a fee of $75, or five installments of $15. In exchange, they received 22 course packets. It was expected that the students would complete the packets in eight to twelve months, although there was no fixed time period. Additionally, students were expected to approach local physicians for some clinical experience, a requirement that seemed to be, at best, encouraged, and at worst, not strictly enforced. Bertha sought out Dr. Sherrill at Camp Crook, South Dakota, not far from the Montana border. In 1918, the average age of the students is stated as 36, so this program was clearly geared towards those whom we now call in higher education "non-traditional students."

Each learning packet at the Chataqua School of Nursing would contain typewritten lectures, several pages long, which were accompanied by illustrations. Students were expected to read these lectures, study them, and then practice the skills in a clinical situation.

Examples of some of the lecture topics are as follows:

- General Surgery operations and Instruments (57 pages, with illustrations)

- Obstetrical/Surgical Nursing: Obstetrical Surgery (42 pages, with illustrations)

- Obstetrical/Surgical Nursing: Labor, Its Physiology and Mechanism, Approach (25 pages with illustrations)

- Dietetics and Invalid Feeding (18 pages, no illustrations)

- Studies in General Nursing: Questions and Problems (19 pages, no illustrations)

- Bandaging (64 pages, with illustrations)

- Surgical Nursing Complications (39 pages, with illustrations)

This is just a small sampling. The research assistant at the National Library of Medicine with whom I spoke speculated that a lot of the students worked already as "semi-trained hospital aides" who were taking the courses to improve their skills and occupational standing, and I am guessing that this may have been the case with Bertha. Because of her later professional activities, it was most probable that she worked as a midwife or nurse's aide of some sort and wished to formalize her education.

In 1925, only one year after beginning her correspondence course in Nursing, and presumably having finished, Bertha purchased "the old Yokely property" and opened the Berry Hospital in Ekalaka, Montana to which, at one time, a large number of Ekalaka's residents could attribute their start in life. It was established primarily as a maternity hospital. In a local history written about Carter County Montana, many residents mention that their children were born at "the Bertha Berry residence" or at "the hospital run by Bertha Berry." From descriptions, it was a large building, originally built as a residence. In Ekalaka, bedridden patients were cared for in the home, since there was no hospital and for years there was no hospital closer than Miles City, some 70 miles away. Ekalaka did have a doctor at various points in its early history, but no hospital until Bertha opened hers. For 17 years, Bertha delivered Ekalaka's babies, until the Berry Maternity Hospital discontinued operation in 1942. At that time, Dahl Memorial Hospital, still in operation today, was built in Ekalaka.

Bertha's daughter Mary Belle, born in 1902 while the family was still in Oklahoma, was Bertha's connection to Tenney, and thus the reason Bertha's name appears on the Tenney quilt. Mary Belle had been working as a beautician in Ekalaka, her home town, when Frank Pithey came to town. Frank was the brother of Linna Pithey Gordhamer, featured in the previous chapter. I don't know what brought Frank to Montana, but it was not uncommon for Midwestern men to head west to find work in the rapidly developing American West. There were many opportunities in farm labor, carpentry, logging, and mining. Frank and Mary Belle courted and were married in Ekalaka, and moved back to Tenney the same year the quilt was made, 1928. They lived for a period of time with Frank's brother Fred Pithey and family in Tenney, then bought their own home in town before settling on a farm, where they stayed for many years. When their health forced them to discontinue farming, Frank and Mary Belle moved to neighboring Campbell, where they operated the Pithey Recreation Parlor.

Bertha had a special place in her heart for new mothers and their babies. She had seen far too many tragic circumstances surrounding childbirth and childhood illnesses, many of which could have been prevented. The Sheppard-Towner Act of 1921 (officially the "Sheppard-Towner Maternity and Infancy Protection Act") was established in reaction to the high infant mortality rate present in the United States. Sara Josephine Baker stated during World War I that "it was six times safer to be a soldier in the trenches than to be born a baby in the United States" (Felder, 1997). The federally funded health care program, often referred to as the first welfare program in the United States, had as its principal goal the reduction of maternal and infant mortality rates. States provided matching funds to put structures in place to teach expectant mothers about disease prevention, personal hygiene, and other prenatal issues. It faced opposition from the start, particularly from the American Medical Association, which objected to the program's administration by a non-medical group, the U.S. Government. By 1929, Congress discontinued the program (Felder, 1997). However, up to that point, there were seminars and baby clinics all across America as a result of this act. Wilkin County Fair flyers of the time advertise free medical exams for each child under age six. In 1928, there was mention in the newspaper about a small group of Tenney women who went to a "baby clinic" in Wahpeton, where their children would get checked for the symptoms of common childhood illnesses. These were typical of the activities promoted by the Sheppard-Towner Act.

A bit of levity is perhaps due, in the form of a tale that—who knows—may be a folk tale, but knowing Tenney's characters of days gone by, just might be fact. It was presented as true in a Waite family history book of stories written by Jean Schwinn, Thomas Waite's great granddaughter (Schwinn, 1984). Thomas and Jennie Waite were early settlers in Tenney, and Jennie's name along with several of her relatives appears on the Tenney Quilt. Thomas built coffins for friends and neighbors who had died, and Jennie's job was to line the coffins with cotton fabric to provide the appearance of comfort for a loved one's final resting place. A hearse, presumably from Campbell, was sent to Fairmount to pick up "Grandpa Nelson," a local resident. A pig which had escaped its pen somewhere along the route became the unfortunate traffic victim of the hearse as it sped along the road. In the case of the hearse vs. pig, the hearse won. The hearse driver, not wishing to leave perfectly good road kill behind, picked up the dead pig and, without any other options at the time, put the messy pig in the hearse, right alongside Mr. Nelson, so the meat would not be wasted. Grandpa Nelson probably would not have minded, but the Nelson family was not only shocked, but quite insulted. I am guessing that the hearse driver quickly got over any consequences and promptly enjoyed the benefit of salt pork, bacon and a variety of pork products for the succeeding months.

Bertha Berry proudly chose to work outside the home, dedicating her life to helping young mothers and their babies. She did this at a time when the societal expectations of women were to rear children, make clothing and household items, keep house, and stay in the background, allowing her husband to shine, She had the resolve to get an education in whatever manner was available to her, and did it at age 47, when most women of her time were considered to be somewhere between the rocking chair and the casket.

Bertha's husband Charles died in1943, when Bertha was 67 years old. She continued to live in Ekalaka until her own death eleven years later at age 77. In 1928, the year the quilt was made, Bertha, at age 51, would have been visiting her daughter Mary Belle Pithey, in Tenney, or perhaps Mary Belle simply put her mother's name on the quilt as a tribute. In any case, through the careful stitching of 11 letters on a piece of white muslin, BERTHA BERRY will forever be woven into the fabric of Tenney, Minnesota, and would represent the newly independent woman of the late 1920s.

CHAPTER 6
- The Factory Workers -

Isabelle

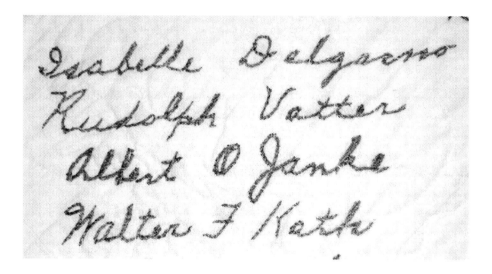

In the summer of 1928, Isabelle Dalgarno was 27 years old and living on a farm in Tenney with her mother and two brothers, about to embark on an adventure that would bring her to the big city of Minneapolis—150 miles to the east—and eventually on to New York City. By early 1929, Isabelle was living in a rooming house on Garfield Avenue in Minneapolis, sharing a room with Agnes Mueller, a 26-year-old widow and a co-worker at the Honeywell factory. Isabelle and Agnes paid a total of $11 a month for their single room in a rooming house. Within the previous year, Isabelle's older sister, Nellie (featured previously), had made her way to Minneapolis and had found employment at the same factory. Isabelle, most likely seeing that there was money to be made in such a venture, followed in her older sister's footsteps; however, they did not live together while in Minneapolis.

Isabelle, born in 1901, was the third child of Nathaniel and Hannah Dalgarno, farmers in Traverse County. Nathaniel had immigrated from Scotland and Hannah, from Sweden. Isabelle appears on the Tenney quilt along with her brothers George and Norman, sister Nellie, and uncle, Alex Dalgarno. Her father, Nathaniel, had died by this time. Alex Dalgarno, born in Scotland, was an unmarried, prosperous farmer in the Tenney area who bred shorthorn cattle on his 320-acre "Willow Grove Stock Farm." Unfortunately, as it turns out, the Depression took its toll on Alex's heirs, as the herd only brought a fraction of what it was worth when Alex died in 1934.

At the turn of the century, as Minneapolis and St. Paul became major manufacturing centers, many young women, especially young first- or second-generation immigrant women such as Isabelle, left their rural homes and moved to these cities to work (Bingham, 1989). Motivated by either the desire for an independent existence or the need to contribute to the family income, these young women often worked for poor wages and lived in harsh conditions, perhaps in a run down rooming house or residence, sharing a bed or a room with others and barely making ends meet. Others were able to find better accommodations and were able to send money back to their families on the farm. It would seem that, at a rent of $11 per month, Isabelle's accommodations would certainly not have been at the higher end of the spectrum. These factory workers often lived in much poorer conditions than those who found jobs as domestic workers, in which the young women lived in the homes of wealthy—or at least "comfortable"—people. These domestics were not paid particularly well, but at least they were able to live in fine homes, had three meals a day, and did not have to worry about working in an unsafe, unhealthy environment. As it would turn out, Isabelle would one day live in the lap of luxury, but for the time being, she and her roommate lived in less than luxurious conditions and supported themselves by doing assembly work in a factory.

Particularly in the garment and knitting factories—but also others—female factory workers were often paid by a piece rate, only making money when they worked very, very fast. Besides creating an environment in which women had to work fast in order to make money, the piecework approach also encouraged them to avoid breaks and to take work home, thus providing a situation that was unhealthy from many perspectives. These women typically worked ten-hour days and worked in dark, stuffy environments that were hot in the summer and cold in the winter. Examples of the types of factory work for which young, rural women went to the City:

- Sewing shirts, suits, overalls, union suits

- Sewing flour sacks and mattresses

- Weaving woolen blankets

- Constructing shoes

- Knitting

- Making cigars

- Making paper boxes

- Bagging seed

- Assembling a variety of products such as, in Isabelle's case, heat regulators

Some of the manufacturers in operation in the Twin Cities during the time Isabelle and Nellie were working in the factories were Munsingwear, North Star Woolen Mills, Minnesota Paints (later, Valspar), Minneapolis Moline, Pure Oil, the Washburn and Pillsbury flour mills, Toastmaster, Northern Ordnance, Northrup King, American Hoist and Derrick, Minnesota Mining and Manufacturing (3M), and a variety of factories related to the lumbering industry—furniture factories, lumber processors, and sash and door factories. This is just a sampling.

Munsingwear is an example of a garment factory in Minneapolis that employed primarily women, but which rose far above many of the others in terms of the environment provided for its employees.

Munsingwear, in fact, was recognized in 1917 for its good working conditions (Premium Wear, Inc., 2006). In 1917, this was a significant recognition, given the conditions for the female workers in many factories of the time. The company's signature product in that era became the cream-colored, one-piece union suit. One-tenth of all U.S. made union suits were produced by Munsingwear and its predominantly female workforce. Big long underwear orders for U.S. troops fighting in the First World War gave the company widespread recognition (Premium Wear, Inc., 2006). Throughout the Twenties, Munsingwear expanded its product line to 102 different styles of underwear, made out of everything from cotton to wool to silk to all sorts of knit and woven fabrics. I can still remember forays to the Munsingwear fabric store in Minneapolis with my mother in the 1960s, where she purchased specialty fabrics for her many sewing projects.

A factory at the other end of the spectrum in terms of working conditions was the Strutwear Knitting Factory. The company, which had started up in 1916, had a long history of anti-labor sentiment and in 1927, the year before the Tenney Quilt, locked out a small number of knitters at its Minneapolis plant because of their labor activity. The factory gained a rather unsavory reputation for its planting of spies to first detect and then restrict labor activity. But that wasn't all. The company then coerced employees to sign contracts from joining labor unions, and the Management fired non-union employees who had family ties to union members (Vaughan, 2002-2003). Women's employment spiked during the World War I years. It declined during the early Twenties, but throughout the Twenties and Thirties, the Minnesota workforce consisted of approximately 20 to 22 percent women (Bingham, 1989). Bingham cites laborsaving devices in the home, as well as new clothing styles which gave more physical freedom, as a few of the many factors which influenced women to work.

However, in spite of increasing opportunities for women in the workforce, women's work was viewed with a sense of "temporaryness," which clustered women into the lower paid, unskilled jobs and in general, devalued women's work. Both employers and male employees tended to view women as marginal and temporary, given that working women generally discontinued their work once they married.

Historian Alice Kessler-Harris, referring to women in the workforce in the Twenties, stated that "Women were invited into the workforce and again invited not to expect too much of it" (Dumenil, 1995).

During the years leading up to Isabelle's employment with the company, the Minneapolis Heat Regulator Company was going to great effort to make itself and its products visible to the American public, particularly Minnesota folks. The company commissioned a well-known Minneapolis artist to create several paintings showing domestic, residential scenes in which the Minneapolis thermostat was prominently visible (Monti, 2007). They were putting the word out that workers were needed to help make these wonderful new devices that would make the lives of Americans comfortable and convenient. It could be that these marketing efforts reached the Dalgarno sisters and influenced their decision to move to Minneapolis to act on this exciting employment possibility.

In 1927, the year before Nellie Dalgarno had arrived at the factory, Minneapolis Heat Regulator Company had merged with the Honeywell Heating Specialty Company of Indiana and made their home base at a new factory at 4th Avenue and 28th Street in Minneapolis. That original factory still serves as the cornerstone for the complex which is now nearly a square city block in size, though the company is no longer headquartered in Minneapolis. The two companies—Minneapolis Heat Regulator and Honeywell—had been each other's primary competitors and had patents which blocked the other from future growth. The merged company was named Minneapolis-Honeywell Regulator Company and, eventually, Honeywell. With the automatic thermostat finally starting to catch on with consumers, the Thirties were Honeywell's initial boom years, and I'd like to think that both Nellie and Isabelle played a part—a small part, but a part nonetheless—in setting the stage for this major surge of success in Honeywell's history.

Isabelle may have traveled to work on the electric streetcar, the City's only source of mass transit in those years—or she may have walked, as her rooming house was about twelve city blocks from the Honeywell facility. Even though electric streetcar service had already started to decrease by the mid-Twenties due to the rising popularity of the automobile, city folks relied on the big, yellow, wooden trolleys until the mid-1950s. Former city dwellers had already started to move out to the suburbs by this time due to the new-found mobility provided by automobiles. It is hard to imagine that, by the late Twenties, the traffic and parking congestion was already a problem on downtown Minneapolis streets. The Minneapolis-St. Paul area of the Twenties was a busy, thriving metropolitan area, ranking 13th in population in the nation by 1930 (Kane, 1983). It was a leading manufacturing center, and a progressive, happening place. But with that progress came poverty, intolerance, and crime. The City opened Isabelle's eyes to a world—good and bad—that she had not experienced back in little Tenney, Minnesota.

It was while she was living in Minneapolis that Isabelle lost her older brother George in a farming accident back in Tenney that was documented in gruesome detail on the front page of the *Breckenridge Gazette* on September 3, 1930. The Dalgarnos were still farming in rural Tenney, with mother Hannah, and brothers George and Norman living on the home place having taken over the farming operation after the death of their father. George had been on the tractor plowing a wheat field. Somehow in the process of shifting the tractor in to or out of gear, it hit a rock precisely at the wrong moment, causing George to fly off the back of the tractor and onto the ground, where he then became pinned underneath the plow. Because George had been at the end of a row, preparing to turn around and head the opposite direction, the steering wheel was cranked into a turning position. As George was pinned below the plow, the tractor disengaged from the plow and kept on moving, in a circular path, leaving George and the plow behind. Badly injured, pinned, and unable to move, George could apparently see the tractor circling around and knew it was headed back in his direction and would most likely hit him again. The tractor did indeed bump against the plow as it circled around and the plow again started to move, dragging George who was still pinned underneath, eventually stopping several yards later. His brother Norman later came looking for George when he did not appear at the dinner table, and furiously dug around the plow in an attempt to free George. Miraculously, George had not been instantly killed, but he did die two days later in the Wheaton Hospital from his injuries. Automobile accidents and farm accidents such as this one tended to be frequent, as well as documented in painful detail in the rural Minnesota newspapers of the time. It is almost as though farmers and others suffered a long adjustment period to the engines, fuel, speed, and power of the technological advances of the time. This event certainly must have been a traumatic one for George's family including sister Isabelle, who was able to leave her factory job only briefly to come home from Minneapolis to attend the funeral, then return immediately.

In the fall of 1930, having made and saved some money by working as a factory assembler, Isabelle made the decision to travel to New York City to visit her aunt, a person whom I only know to be "Mrs. Benson." This was presumably one of her mother's sisters, as I learned through earlier newspaper accounts that Isabelle's mother, Hannah Dalgarno, had made at least a few trips to New York City to visit family members in previous years. Isabelle's visit with her aunt in New York City in 1930 would prove to be a turning point in her life.

Isabelle's east coast visit not only provided a wonderful opportunity to see her mother's extended family, but it somehow connected her with a wealthy family who subsequently offered her a position in their home. Isabelle accepted the position, and left Honeywell's heat regulators far behind. I do not know the details of the position, but Isabelle worked as some sort of domestic aide, a position which may have included any of the domestic tasks such as helping with children, laundry, cleaning, cooking, gardening, or any number of other household tasks. Depending on the wealth of the family for whom she worked and thus, the number of domestic workers they hired, Isabelle could have either focused primarily on one of these tasks, or helped with all of them. At any rate, she apparently worked in one of New York City's finest homes, according to Isabelle's obituary. I unfortunately have not been able to determine exactly which family Isabelle served or where they lived; but I do know that Isabelle had endeared herself to this wealthy family. This chance opportunity became, for Isabelle, the door to what she would have considered at the time to be a very good life.

Unfortunately, Isabelle's life would take another unexpected turn.

In the summer of 1934, having been in New York City for four years, Isabelle began to have increasing trouble with her throat. It had been a slight bother before that point, but things were getting worse. So she had surgery in August of that year to remove her tonsils—a considerably more complicated and risk-laden surgery than it has become today—and had planned to go back to Minnesota to rest and recuperate. But Isabelle seemingly recuperated more quickly than anticipated right there in New York City, so decided not to make the long train trip home to Minnesota. She had informed her Minnesota family that she was doing well, and though they would have loved to see her, they were relieved that all was well and that she was strong enough to go back to work. Isabelle's employer family was understanding, and saw that she was well cared for. Additionally, Isabelle's aunt, cousin, and other relatives provided whatever extra support was needed until she could return to her job duties. It was understandably with much shock and sorrow that the Dalgarnos read the telegram in late November notifying them that Isabelle had suddenly died.

Since the tonsillectomy, as well as before the surgery, Isabelle had been troubled with throat pain and constriction, sometimes more sometimes less, but had always been able to continue her job duties with her New York family. Suddenly in late November of 1934, Isabelle became quite ill with this throat malady and was hospitalized. Her employer, apparently of great financial means, brought in eight different doctors to consult on Isabelle's case. Yet none of them was able to diagnose just what was happening, thus none of them knew how to treat her. Everything possible was done for Isabelle under the circumstances, including three blood transfusions, but to no avail. The telegram received by her mother to notify her of Isabelle's death simply stated that Isabelle had died of an incurable throat ailment. All told, her final illness and hospitalization was only five days in duration. Isabelle's body was shipped back to Minnesota on the train, accompanied by the aunt whom she originally went to visit. Her funeral was held in the Swedish Lutheran church in Wheaton, where Isabelle's mother had been comforted for several years among the company of other Swedish immigrants.

As I reflect on the various tragedies that had befallen so many of the families of my Tenney women, the need for the support that a small town like Tenney could provide is quite evident. And the support indeed was there—for Isabelle's mother, and for those before and after her. The lives of Tenney people, by virtue of the smallness of the world in that time, were intertwined in ways that lives no longer intertwine. Women were nurturers not only of their own family, but of their community. The Tenney women took care of their own. Upon the news of a death or tragedy of some sort in the family, the women were right there—Johnny on the spot—with food, words of condolence and encouragement, and invitations to take care of the children and the laundry in their own homes. They sat with the sick, cleaned wounds, delivered babies, made pots of soup, and prepared bodies for the undertaker. The men banded together to take care of field work, milk cows, and take care of the stock. As a Minnesotan, I am proud that we tend to still rally around those in need with kind words, offers of future help, and gifts of something Minnesotans know a lot about: "hotdishes." But the world in which neighbors truly *take care of* neighbors seems to have gone to the same place where the daily recitation of the "Pledge of Allegiance" went.

Isabelle's mother, a widow, had now lost four important people in her life in a relatively short period of time. She had lost her husband a few years prior, then her son, George, in the terrible farm tractor accident. Three years later, she took in to her home her bachelor brother-in-law, Alex Dalgarno, and nursed him for six months through an illness that finally took his life. Now, just six months after Alex's death, she received the word that her youngest child, age 33, had died. Hannah Dalgarno, sadly, was really quite typical of women of her time and thus, of my Tenney women. The progression of their life stories is marked with the tragedies brought on by the technological infancy of the times in which they lived. Babies and mothers died in childbirth, children suffered horribly and died of diseases that have now become medical non-events, and even Mother Nature seemed to strike greater severity and frequency. Accidents maimed or killed loved ones. Through all of these things, women persevered and stood firm in their faith. How often have we heard our mothers, aunts, grandmothers and if lucky enough, our great grandmothers, say, "It is so."

This is the wonderful gift of strength and steadfastness that the women role models in our lives have given to us and that we must pass along to our daughters.

I feel that I have come to know Isabelle, even though I was not able to talk with anyone who knew her well so that I could capture, in words, her true heart and soul. But she is a friend, by proxy, and her story deserves to be told. Of all my Tenney women, Isabelle is the one with whom I most closely identify. Had I lived in Tenney at the time, I know that she and I would have been friends. I would have been at the Tenney train depot with her, waiting to board a train to Minneapolis to see the big city and to live independently. My glance back at my dusty little town of Tenney would have been tender, but fleeting. "I'll be back," she would have said, "but only to visit." Our work ethics would have made Isabelle and me the fastest, most efficient thermostat assemblers at Honeywell, and we would have made as much money as we could so that we could move on to the next adventure. Then, restless and excited, I would have stood right beside her on the platform at the Union Train Station in Minneapolis, waiting for the train to New York City, excitedly contemplating the place where the streets never end and people never sleep. We would have been thirsty for the new experiences that New York City would have provided us, and we would have told about them in great detail and enthusiasm in our letters home. I would have shared in her excitement as she was offered a job in one of New York City's finest homes, and dreamed with her about where it would lead. In the end, I would have been devastated to learn that something had gone terribly wrong, and that even the best medical care available in New York City would not be enough to save her life. So I would have proudly gotten on that train and accompanied Isabelle on her long ride home from New York City to her final resting place. Isabelle's work ethic, her sense of self and strength of character, molded by the example set by her mother, served Isabelle well in her short life.

Isabelle left Tenney full of ambition and promise and adventure. Circumstances beyond her control dictated that she would never return to the place that gave birth to her adventurous spirit—Tenney, Minnesota.

CHAPTER 7

- The Seamstresses -

Marie

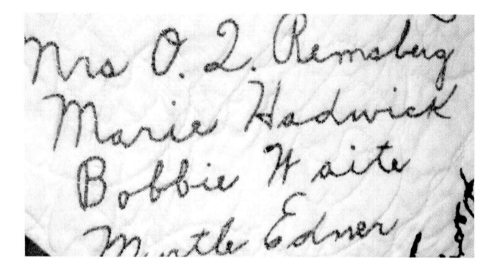

In 1928, Marie Hadwick was living alone, divorced, in Campbell and working independently as a seamstress out of her home. Marie had been born in Waupaca, Wisconsin in 1880 to James Swan, a Canadian, and wife Elizabeth, from Wales. She had made, like so many Wilkin County residents, a journey that began in Wisconsin and progressed with her family westward, eventually to Minnesota, as land or jobs became available. Marie's family took a roundabout way to get there, but did indeed eventually land in Minnesota.

The Swan family had immigrated to the United States from Canada, making their way originally to Bellville, Kansas, where James was a farm laborer. Marie's two older sisters, Charlotte and Fannie, were born while the family lived in Kansas. They all, then, moved to Waupaca, Wisconsin, where Marie, a younger brother Thomas, and a younger sister, Beth, were born. In 1896, the family made one final move, to Campbell, Minnesota. Exactly what brought the family to Campbell remains a mystery, though as we have discovered, a large number of families from Wisconsin moved west to the Tenney and Campbell area. Certainly the Swans would have known others from their area of Wisconsin who had settled in Wilkin County and perhaps were lured there by its lush Red River Valley soil. Like so many others, however, dreams died prematurely, as Marie's father, James, passed away within only a few years of arriving in Campbell, sometime in the four-year period of time between 1896 and 1900. During that time, Marie, the oldest child at home, was trained as a school teacher and was hired to teach in one of the rural schools surrounding Campbell.

The 1900 census showed mother Elizabeth as living in Campbell with three children—Marie (age 20), Thomas (age 16), and Beth (age 13). Marie, though living in Campbell, was well known in Tenney, as were most Campbell people. With the two communities being only five miles apart, Tenney and Campbell were intertwined in many ways, so it is not surprising that Marie's name appears on the Tenney Quilt, as do many other Campbell residents. Marie's later occupation as a seamstress also provided a means of interaction with many Tenney people through the work she did for them.

The man that I believe to be Marie's future husband, Richard Hadwick, came to Campbell sometime around 1900. Richard Hadwick was the only person with that surname to appear in the Wilkin County area (Campbell, in particular) during the period of time that Marie's name changed to Hadwick. I have not been able to find a marriage record of the two, and the two were not married long enough to be recorded in any given census year, so it is a bit more difficult to confirm. However, they were in the same age range, they were both of Scottish or Welsh descent, Richard was the only Hadwick in the area, and it is clear from later census records that both had only been married a brief period of time. I am therefore drawing the conclusion from the information I have that Richard Hadwick was the man to whom Marie was briefly married.

Richard was living in the Pacific House, a hotel, at the turn of the century, working as a barber. This provided an opportunity to meet Marie, who also lived in Campbell at the time, working as a school teacher. Perhaps Marie and Richard were attracted to each other because of their common Scottish descent. There were a few other Scottish families in the Tenney and Campbell area at the time—the Dalgarnos, the Dalzeils, Winnifred Davison, the Irvines, the Watsons—but not exactly a large pool from which to choose a husband if Marie or her family felt strongly about such things.

Campbell was a railroad town, the first in the county. The first pieces of railroad track laid by the Minnesota and Pacific hit Campbell in 1870. Building the railroad required about 1,000 logs per mile. That's a lot of labor. A temporary camp was established in Campbell for the next two years, then it moved on to Doran and finally, to Breckenridge, and eventually became what was known as the Great Northern Railroad. Campbell, for a period of time, because of its railroad camp and because the railroad had reached the town, was a hustling, bustling place. But even before the railroad came through, Campbell had established itself as a major stop on the stage line between St. Cloud, Minnesota and Fort Abercrombie, North Dakota, on the Red River of the North. Campbell provided a good night's sleep, a rest for the horses, and a place to get provisions for the remainder of the journey. The Campbell Hotel was frequented by many travelers in the mid to late 19th century.

Many young men came to town during these years to work on the railroad or to work in businesses that were secondary to the railroad camp. Breckenridge, once the railroad reached that town, would steal Campbell's thunder and become the major trade center of the region. The Minnesota and Pacific Railroad arrived in Breckenridge in 1871, and the Northern Pacific Fergus Falls and Black Hills Railroad in 1882. Along with Breck's location on the Red River of the North, this gave Breckenridge all it needed to become a major distributing point—both outgoing and incoming. Agricultural products, primarily wheat, could be shipped out, and needed items—machinery, wood, provisions—could be shipped in. The time period following the arrival of the railroads was a period of rapid growth for the city.

Campbell's railroad was well-established by the time Richard Hadwick came to town right at the turn of the century, negating the possibility that Richard came to town as a railroad laborer. However, Campbell's large hotel, which also served as a boarding house, seemed to attract a certain number of young single men as laborers of various sorts. Seemingly with no other connection to Campbell, Richard came to town with some barbering skills, and apparently found work as a barber, at least long enough to court and marry Miss Marie Swan. This time period in which Richard lived in Campbell could have been as short as one year or as long as six to eight years. Richard and Marie's marriage would have occurred sometime between 1900 and 1908, with Marie in the age range of 20 to 28 and Richard five years older.

Marie apparently did not continue teaching after her marriage, typical of young female teachers of her era as we have found with several other of our Tenney girls. All references to Marie from the time of her marriage, whether in census information or oral history, refer to Marie as a seamstress, a job that was often done out of the woman's home, and was considered "women's work" – therefore socially acceptable.

The marriage of Marie and Richard seemingly was not made in heaven, if based on longevity. The 1910 census shows an already-married-but-now-single Marie Hadwick, living, along with her mother, with the Albert and Fanny Stoebe family in Campbell. Fannie was Marie's older sister. Marie was reported as "widowed" on this 1910 census, perhaps as a result of the shame associated with divorce, but later census records show that she had indeed been divorced. If her husband indeed was Richard, and I certainly believe it was, he was clearly alive and well and living in St. Paul in the years after the marriage.

Once married and then divorced, Marie made her living as a seamstress, working out of her home and sometimes staying in others' homes while sewing clothing for the family. Ray Gore, my great great uncle, was a large man, and appreciated good quality suits and coats. Because he was unable to easily find the size and type of clothing he wanted, he called on Marie to make quite a bit of his clothing, including trousers, suits, and overcoats. While working on Mr. Gore's cloth-ing, Marie stayed with Ray and his wife Vesta so that Marie would have constant access to Ray in order to try on the clothing and make adjustments or alterations as she progressed. Marie also did quite a bit of sewing for the George Edner family. Muriel Lee Edner (now Fagan) vividly recalls Marie Hadwick and her mother sitting and sew-ing together, as one cut and one sewed, making snow suits and wool pants for Muriel Lee's younger brothers, Garth and Jerry.

Most women of the time sewed out of necessity, relying on their own resourcefulness to create not only articles of clothing, but house-hold items. For example, unbleached flour sacks could easily be made into dish towels, which were then hemmed and embroidered. Or they could be made into curtains or pieced quilts. Personal items such as underwear, night clothes, and petticoats could also be crafted from flour sacks. Clothing from older children, no matter what the condi-tion, was either used by younger children "as is" with a few patches here and there, or remade into something smaller and more usable. If an item was unusable as clothing, into the rag bag it would go, along with the holey socks and underwear and other items—clean, but no longer fit for wear. In their next life these scraps turned in to piece quilts, pillows, lap robes, rugs, or even filler for appliquéd items. When a dress was no longer wearable, it could be remade into a dress for a child in the household. When it was anything other than plain cotton or cotton print, it was considered a very special dress to a young girl. Nothing was wasted.

Though many, if not most, articles of clothing were hand-sewn in the Twenties, Thirties and Forties, the Montgomery Ward catalog was a source of clothing for many people in Tenney. My mother remem-bers receiving clothing from the Montgomery Ward catalog as a child. Montgomery Ward had been in the mail order catalog business since 1872, and by 1928 had over 500 stores across the country (Wikimedia Foundation Inc., 2007), providing a practical means of shopping be-fore the full mobilization of rural Minnesotans. Sears also had a large mail order catalog business but didn't seem to enjoy the popularity of Montgomery Ward among Tenney folks.

A day trip to Breckenridge could also provide most shopping

needs of most Tenney people. It did have its drawbacks, however. One day later much later in Tenney, school teachers Irene Doyle and Doris Raguse, went on a Breckenridge shopping outing, inviting Florence Doleman to accompany them. The unfortunate part of this whole incident is that Irene and Doris forgot Florence in Breckenridge, and didn't even realize it until they were back in Tenney. They just plain forgot her there. So of course, realizing their mistake, they turned around and drove the twenty miles back to Breckenridge which, would have probably meant about a 40-minute drive by the time they got to wherever they left Florence.

Florence was there, waiting.

Apparently it wasn't pretty.

One would have to believe that the icy silence in the car on the way back to Tenney was rather awkward. Florence's grandson Neil reports that Florence and the Doyles never really got along after that. The moral of the story: If you're going to forget someone somewhere, try to remember this fact before you get all the way back to Tenney.

When his marriage with Marie ended, Richard moved to St. Paul and lived in a boarding house on College Avenue, continuing to work as a barber. He remarried, but lost his second wife, Mollie, to illness in 1929. He continued to work as a barber his entire adult life, until his death in 1942 in St. Paul.

Back in Campbell, Marie never married again. Apparently her experience with Richard, whatever it was—and I imagine I will never know—cured her urge to ever marry again. Or perhaps it was simply a matter of the eligible bachelor pool being considerably decreased for an "older" divorced woman of the time. Marie lived together with her mother, Elizabeth Swan, until Elizabeth died in 1920 of Bright's Disease. So at the time of the quilt, Marie had been living alone for eight years. She never left Wilkin County. From Campbell, she moved to Breckenridge in approximately 1930, where she continued to work as a seamstress, again out of her home. She led an active social life, attending birthday parties and other celebrations back in her home territory of Campbell and Tenney. Her name was mentioned frequently in accounts of ladies aid meetings, card clubs, coffee parties, church events, and town celebrations. In addition, once Marie moved to Breckenridge, her work brought her back "home" frequently, as she stayed in various homes in Tenney and Campbell as she worked on sewing and mending projects. Marie passed away in 1957 at the age of 77 years.

Many Tenney and Campbell people remember Marie as a quiet, sensible person and a very capable seamstress. Very often women worked as seamstresses and dressmakers out of the town's general mercantile or, if the town was big enough, out of a storefront which would sometimes also house a milliner. This was not the case in Campbell, with Marie working independently in her home. However, apparently Mrs. O.J. (Alice) Edner, whose name also appears on the Tenney Quilt, worked as a milliner at the turn of the century out of their family general store, the O.J. Edner Store, in Campbell.

Throughout history, sewing has been a thread, pardon the pun, that has tied women together. No matter what the social or economic status, ethnicity, religion, or educational level, women have sewn. Sewing has always served as a useful and necessary activity for the creation of clothing and household articles, and could be done with a group of women or alone. In the eighteenth, nineteenth and early twentieth centuries, it was one of the few means through which women were allowed creative freedom, and was viewed by society as a valuable skill. Sewing was a socially acceptable means of getting together with other women, allowing women to have social relationships independent of their husbands or other family members. Whereas professional pursuits were not always looked upon favorably, sewing was always acceptable, as were other domestic jobs such as taking in laundry, taking in boarders, or working in another family's home as a "domestic." Few expanded their sewing to the professional level like Marie Hadwick, but in Marie's case it was a skill that she used her entire life in order to make a living.

However, at the same time sewing, in a sense, held women "in their place." An interesting parallel is presented by Rozsika Parker in her book *The Subversive Stitch*. She asks readers to compare the image of a woman doing handwork or needlework of any sort to her historical position in relation to man. Her eyes are lowered, her head is bent down and her shoulders are hunched. It is a picture of repression—subjugation—silence. So, while the needle arts have provided a source of pleasure and power for women, these activities are "indissolubly linked to their powerlessness" (Parker, 1989). An extreme feminist viewpoint? Perhaps so, perhaps not. In any case, it is an interesting observation.

"Quilt." Just the mention of the word evokes a sense of comfort—home—grandmothers—warmth—and all things good. The quilting tradition that led to the creation of the Tenney Quilt in 1928 was long and colorful and requires a much larger discussion than this venue allows. What is more relevant to this text is the role that quilting played in the lives of women of that time period. Quilting meant much more than just making blankets.

The act of getting together to make a quilt has served as an important social opportunity for women for generations. Traditional quilting is a team sport. Unlike other women's handcrafts such as knitting or tatting or embroidery, quilting provided a socially acceptable means for women to gather together in close proximity and speak freely. We take for granted today the opportunity to simply express our opinions when, in 1928, women were only beginning to emerge from a time, in rural Minnesota, when that was not acceptable in a public setting. As their fingers and needles were busy working on the quilt, the women talked about child care and housekeeping hints, the latest products available for housewives, marital relations, medical advice, community happenings, politics, births, deaths, weddings, religion, world happenings, and town gossip. Women could support each other, offer each other advice, and share recipes, patterns, and home remedies. Quilting provided a venue to enjoy the companionship of friends simply by virtue of the process required to put a quilt together. Two or three or four or more sets of hands were better than one, and those hands were connected to intelligent, creative women who, just like you and me, had a lot to offer the world, but not too many venues through which it could be offered.

In the case of the Tenney quilt, the act of sitting together and embroidering the names onto the quilt squares would have provided this opportunity. The Tenney Quilt was, however, unique from many quilting experiences of the day in that the women did not hand-stitch the quilt together, as most would have done in that era. Instead, they embroidered the names and designs, sewed the quilt squares together, and then sent it off to Dayton's Department Store in Minneapolis to machine-stitch the layers together. Dayton's had opened its doors 26 years earlier and was one of the four major department stores in downtown Minneapolis at the time of the quilt, along with Powers, Donaldson's and Young Quinlan. I have tried unsuccessfully to solve the mystery as to why the Tenney women would have decided to send the quilt off to Minneapolis to be commercially stitched, and where the connection with Dayton's Department Store existed. I suppose that will remain a mystery. However, despite the fact that the Tenney women did not sit together and hand-stitch the quilt, the communal nature of quilting was very evident throughout the quilt's creation. A community fundraising quilt becomes a communal process by virtue of its purpose.

This communal nature of quilting, and the bonds that quilting created and reinforced, paralleled a societal trend that had been emerging since the First World War. Women found that by bonding together they had more power and a bit more control over their world and thus, their lives. The women's suffrage movement which culminated in the right to vote in 1920 was, of course, a prime example.

Women used quilts to change the world around them. During the First World War, women were encouraged to make their own home bedding so that commercially-made blankets could go overseas (Lasansky). In this way quilting became a way for women to collectively help the war effort using the skills that were socially acceptable for them. Another example was the use of fundraising quilts, of which the Tenney Quilt is an example. The creation of fundraising quilts began in the mid-nineteenth century, with the funds mostly used for various church needs (Marx Atkins, 1984). Such examples might be to pay off church repairs or maintenance, or perhaps to contribute to the building of a new church, or even catch up on the minister's salary. More commonly they were used to support missions and other humanitarian causes. This tradition of using quilts to support benevolence activities continues today even in my own church and many others, particularly in the Midwest, where quilts are made and given to families who have lost homes to fires or natural disasters, or to those going through other traumatic life events.

Fundraising quilts generally fell into two major categories, subscription quilts and tithing quilts (Marx Atkins, 1984). The Tenney Quilt is an example of a subscription quilt, in which money was gathered from individuals or businesses whose names were then embroidered or otherwise recognized somehow on the quilt, and the money used for a specific project. The other type, tithing or revenue quilts, were tied directly to the church, listing the names of members who promised specific amounts to support the church, with the money used strictly for church-related projects. Names were more often embroidered, as they were on the Tenney Quilt, than written in ink. Sometimes the arrangement of the names provided the entire design of the quilt; in other cases such as the Tenney Quilt, it consisted mostly of names, but also included some other design element. In our Tenney Quilt, this design element included flower baskets in a simple redwork design. Flower baskets became popular quilt images right about this time in quilting history.

Marx Atkins states that, before the turn of the century, fundraising quilts were generally raffled once completed, providing an additional source of money for the designated project. However, in conservative circles raffles were sometimes viewed as a form of gambling or playing a game of chance. Some groups got around this "technicality" by offering a piece of gum or other small token item along with the raffle ticket. This way, they could claim that the purchaser of the raffle ticket was actually buying a product, not gambling. The other option was to hold an auction to sell the quilt to the highest bidder. In some cases the quilt, once completed, and the money having been collected for the signatures, was given to the person who had devoted the most energy to the fundraising effort.

I wish I knew the details regarding the final disposition of the Tenney Quilt—how did the Tenney women determine who would be its owner? Because my great aunt LaVanche organized this fundraising project and eventually ended up as the owner of the finished quilt, it would seem logical that the last option is a possibility, i.e., she, as the organizer was presented the quilt in appreciation for her efforts.

However, an equally logical possibility that I have mentioned previously is that LaVanche, because she was a gainfully employed, independent young woman, could have simply bid the highest bid at an auction. I hope to someday learn the full story, but with the passage of time, the chances of learning the story get slimmer and slimmer.

The TENNEY QUILT—just a blanket? Not to me. The quilt could easily have landed on someone's bed, worn to shreds through the years, and eventually relegated to the garbage can. I am guessing that would have been just fine with the Tenney women who made it, given their frugality and their impassioned desire that nothing go to waste. How glad I am, however, that my great aunt LaVanche had the foresight as a young woman to put the quilt in a trunk and carefully preserve it so that I, two generations removed, would one day enjoy it and learn from it. This is a historical document, written in one of the only ways that the writing of history could have been accomplished by the women of Tenney. Their needles became their pens and the Tenney Quilt, their "eminently expressive text" (Ferrero, Hedges and Silber).

At a personal level, the Tenney Quilt is representative of the women who paved my way. They lived lives that would turn most of us to mush. Many immigrated to this country, having to learn a new language, adjust to a new world, find a new support system, and literally build new lives from the ground up. And the second-generation immigrants still had to endure hardships that we can only imagine— the untimely deaths of children, husbands, and siblings; horrendous drought and blizzards, extreme heat and extreme cold; unimaginable living and working conditions; and household tasks that made every single day a challenge. Through these challenges they still helped others, kept faith, and found joy.

Through this journey I have come to appreciate the energy and fortitude that Octavia brought to Tenney as a young teacher, as well as her adventurous spirit. I am inspired by the mature, intelligent way in which Linna mentored her country school teachers, with seemingly just the right mix of firmness and gentleness. And I am in awe of her lifelong commitment to children of all shapes, sizes, temperaments, and circumstances. I admire Violet's desire to take care of the less fortunate, and Bertha's willingness to not only seek an education during a time when it was unusual for women of her era, but to seek it at age 47. I am inspired by her relentless advocacy for healthy mothers and babies. Nellie was willing to go out and give the greater world a try, yet she stepped back when she realized that "back home" was the best place for her. Knowing when to step back takes a strong person. The unconditional love that my beloved grandmother Audrey gave to me, no matter what, will forever be a model for me as I now seek to be that kind of grandmother to my own grandchildren. And LaVanche's legacy is one of enthusiastic love of life and persistence in all matters, personal or professional. I found, in Isabelle, a kindred adventurous spirit. Lizzie's legacy was her devotion to her child, a legacy that I hope to leave, above almost all else. Likewise, I am inspired by Gertie's unending devotion to her family and her church, as well as her work ethic and her constantly busy hands. And Marie represents one of my most important values—steadiness.

As I stand on that Tenney sidewalk now, the spaces where buildings once stood and people once walked have come alive. The Tenney women who meticulously stitched names onto a quilt in 1928 have turned a lonely, beige landscape into a bright, colorful portrait that I can now carry with me long after Tenney draws its final breath.

APPENDIX

Where is Tenney?

• On Minnesota State Highway 55, about one mile east of the intersection of Minnesota Highway 75 (north-south) and Highway 55 (east-west)

• 7 miles from the Minnesota-North Dakota border, just north of the "bump" on Minnesota's western border

• In the Red River Valley

• 167 miles west of Minneapolis-St. Paul, Minnesota

• 64 miles south of Fargo, North Dakota

It has the distinction of being the smallest town in the State of Minnesota, with a population, at the last census, of six people

Alphabetical List of Names Appearing on the Tenney Quilt

- A -
Ackerman, A.
Albrecht, L.B.
Anderson, G.O. (maybe Gust)
Anderson, Martha
Arensen, Fred
Ashley, Bob
Askegaard, Octavia (later McGregor)

- B -
Ballard, Mrs. G.E.
Berry, Mrs. Charles (Bertha)
Bjornson, Irene
Block, Freda
Boek (possibly Boeck), Gus
Boe, M.A.
Bostrum, John
Boyce, Dinty (possibly Claude)
Boyce, Elsie (married to Dinty)
Boyd, Audrey (later Tiron)
Boyd, Harry
Boyd, Margaret (later Dawson)
Brackin, Ada (Mrs. Theodore)
Brewster, Florence (Mrs. Paul)
Briggs, Bessie (Mrs. Frank)
Brown, Bertha (Mrs. Max)
Brown, Max
Bruce, Irene (Mrs. Elmer)
Burfiand, Eloise
Burhans, Kirk

Byrne, Blanche

- C -
Campasu(?), M.G.
Campbell, Mabel (Mrs. Thomas)
Carlson, Charlotte
Carlson, Ellen (Mrs. Erick)
Carlson, Erick
Carlson, Mabel
Carnes, Elizabeth Sr.
Carnes, Elizabeth Jr.
Carnes, N.K. Sr.
Carnes, N.K. Jr.
Caron, Bernita
Chamberlain, Irene (Mrs. O.C.)
Chamberlain, Ocee
Chambers, Emma (Mrs. Joseph)
Christensen, Anna
Clarey, Fred
Clarey, Matilda (Mrs. Fred)
Cook, Alice
Cross, Barnhard (B.T.)
Cross, Jennie (Mrs. B.T.)
Cross, Jennie
Cross, Jessie
Cross, William
Cummings, E.G.
Cummings, Mrs. E.G.
Cummings, Lucile

- D -
Dalgarno, Alex
Dalgarno, Isabellele
Dalgarno, Nellie (later Dopp)
Dalgarno, Norman
Dalziel, Mrs. Alex
Davison, Clarence
Davison, Ray

Davison, Helen (Mrs. Ray)
Davison, Winnifred (Mrs. Clarence)
Dawson, Howard
Dawson, Florence (Mrs. Jerome)
Dawson, Jerome
Dawson, Lloyd
Dawson, Madge (Mrs. Lloyd)
Dawson, Lillian
Dawson, Robert
Dawson, Samuel Northcraft
Dawson, Kate (Mrs. Samuel)
Dawson, Virginia
DeLoss, Hattie
Dolby, B.T.
Donley, Clarence
Dopp, George
Dunton, Billy
Dunton, Buster
Dunton, Frances
Durner, Archie
Durner, Alice (Mrs. Archie)
Durner, Christine
Durner, Darwin
Durner, Edna (Mrs. John)
Durner, John A.
Durner, Rose (later Murphy)

- E -
Echternach, Myrtle
Edner, Alice (Mrs. O.J.)
Edner, George
Edner, Muriel Lee
Edner, Myrtle (Mrs. George)
Elfstrom, Ruby

Ellis, Harold
Ellis, Fannie (Mrs. Harold)
Engfer, George
Engfer, Mae (Mrs. George)

- F -

Farnsworth, Mrs. D.K.
Fergerson, Ethel
Foat, Mrs.
Funkhouser, Blanche

- G -

Garske, Anna (Mrs. Max)
Garske, Max
Garske, Irvin
Giddings, Harry
Giddings, Stella
Gill, Ed
Gill, Estella (Mrs. Ed)
Gill, Glen
Gill, Grace (later Payne)
Gill, Lloyd
Gill, Melvin
Gill, Roscoe
Gillaspey, Lester
Gillaspey, Lillian
Gillaspey, Marvin
Gillaspey, Violet
Glock, Al
Glock, Ed
Glock, Ernie
Glock, Francis (Mrs. Joseph)
Glock, Jack (John)
Glock, Laura
Glock, Margaret
Glock, Ralph
Goodhue, A.B.
Gordhamer, Clarence
Gordhamer, Linna (Mrs. Clarence)
Gore, Betty (later Clark, Wright)
Gore, Donald
Gore, Geneva (later

Hicks)
Gore, Howard
Gore, Ray
Gore, Vesta (Mrs. Ray)
Gore, Walter
Gore, Belle (Mrs. Walter)
Gran, Elaine
Gran, Gladys
Green, Mrs. Lula
Green, Melba
Greenman, Dr. N.H.
Griffin, Lorna
Griffin, Ruth

- H -

Hadwick, Marie
Hage, Thelma
Hamann, Earl
Hamann, Edith
Hamann, Elsie (Mrs. Norbert)
Hamann, Lena (later O'Keefe)
Hamann, Laura
Hamann, Mary
Hamann, Margaret
Hamann, Opal
Hamann, Otto
Hamann, Cora (Mrs. Otto)
Hanberg (Hamberg?), Esther
Hannon, James
Hanrahan, John
Hanson, Hilda
Hasse, Albert
Hasse, Christina
Hasse, Fred
Hasse, Hermanda
Hasturn (?), Lester
Heald, Helen
Heins, Mae
Hemmerling, Albert
Hemmerling, Jake
Henke, G.O.
Henke, Mrs. G.O.

Henrich, Opal
Hess, Helen Jane
Hinz, Rusty
Hinz, Schimmel
Hoban, Helen
Hofstedt, Albin
Humke, Elizabeth "Lizzie" (later Neisess)
Hungerford, Albert
Hunt, Mrs. Frank
Huse, Clarence

- I -

Iler, Annie Pearl (later Fonnest)
Iler, Lillian
Iler, Sam
Iler, Ruby (Mrs. Sam)

- J -

Jacklitch, Ernest
Jacklitch, Verna (Mrs. Ernest)
Jacklitch, Oscar
Janke, Albert
Janke, Ann (later Plummer)
Janke, Ardis
Janke, Augusta (Mrs. Gust)
Janke, Gust
Janke, Arlene (Mrs. Clifford)
Janke, Clifford
Janke, Mrs. Dan
Janke, Doris (later Schuster, Wawars)
Janke, Herbert
Janke, James
Janke, Mrs. Jim
Janke, Lois
Janke, Mabel
Janke, Myrtle (Mrs. Fred)
Janke, Robert
Jenks, Madge
Johanson, A.R.
Johnson, Arthur

Johnson, Florence
Johnson, Janice
Johnson, Pearl
Johnson, Susie
Johnson, Vernie
Johnston, Mrs. Robert
Jones, Eli
Jones, Amy
Jones, Ella
Jones, Lulu
Jones, May
Juhl, Delphia
Juhl, Rudolph
- **K** -
Kahlhamer, Nandlin
Kapitan, Adeline
Kapitan, Everett
Kapitan, Gert (Mrs. Matthew)
Kapitan, Matthew
Kapitan, Warren
Kath, Albert
Kath, Anna (Mrs. Walter)
Kath, Walter F.
Kath, Annie (Mrs. William)
Kath, William
Kath, Edna (Mrs. Arthur)
Kath, Clarence
Kath, Ernest
Kath, H.F.
Kath, Harold
Kath, Mrs. L.W.
Kath, Leona
Kath, Leonhard
Kath, Lloyd
Kath, Lydia (Mrs. Richard)
Kath, Richard
Kath, Melvin
Kath, Olga
Kath, Paul
Kath, Clara (Mrs. Paul)
Kath, Reinhard
Kath, Verna

Kath, Victor
Keller, Otto
Kerch, Edna
Kloss, August
Kloss, Gusta
Klugman, Dorothy
Klugman, Ida (Mrs. Gust)
Kraemer, Henry
Krinke, Elsie
Kroehler, Anita
Kroehler, Grace
Kroehler, Helen
Kroehler, John Franklin
Kuehl, Lydia
Kuehl, O.A.
Kuentzel, Florene
Kuentzel, Agnes (Mrs. Howard)
Kuentzel, Howard
- **L** -
Larson, A.N.
Larson, Andrew
Larson, Keith
Larson, Ralph
Lee, Charles
Lee, Mrs. Charles
Lester, L. Eugene
Lyngaas, Matilda (Mrs. Lars)
Listhard, Mrs. S.
Litschauer, John
Lodahl, Clarence
Lodahl, Ida (Mrs. Clarence)
Loop, L.L.
Lundhagen, Oscar
- **M** -
Mann, Lena (Mrs. Henry)
Manthie, Alfred
Manthie, Gust
Manthie, Sarah
Marsh, Margaret (Mrs. Harlon)
Max, Ann (later Wood)
Max, J. (Johanna?)

Max, Joe
Max, Lea
Max, Pete
McAlpin, Edward
McAlpin, Kate (Mrs. William)
McCoy, Beulah (later Gill)
McIntyre (later Vertin)
Mellon, Miriam (Mrs. Glen)
Mertes, Elmer
Metcalf, Francis
Metcalf, Marie
Metcalf, Evaline
Miller, Minor
Miller, Mrs. Minor
Miller, S.I.
Minikus, George
Monson, Bernice
Monson, Deloris
Monson, Emma (Mrs. Herbert)
Monson, Gladys
Monson, Tage
Moon, Earl
Moon, Malissa (Mrs. Earl)
Moon, Harley
Moon, Marie
Muellenbach, Albert L.
Mullen, Alice
Mullen, Charles
Mullen, Marvin
Mullen, Mona
Muller, A.B.
Muller, Bob
Muller, Kathrine
Muller, Lauren
Murphy, Pat (real name Allen)
- **N** -
Nadeau, Bertha (Mrs. Frank)
Nadeau, Frank

Neisess, Belle (later Preputin)
Neisess, John
Neisess, Sabina (Mrs. John)
Neisess Florence (Mrs. Albert)
Neisess, Mrs. J.T.
Neumann, Bob
Neumann, Henry
Neumann, Mrs. Henry
Niss, Lawrence
Niss, Leora
Noffsinger, Nora (Mrs. Winfield)
Noffsinger, Winfield "Winnie"
Norton, Mrs. Wallace
Novak, Fritz (Frank)

- O -
O'Brian, W.J.
O'Keefe, Joseph
O'Laughlin, Jack
O'Laughlin, Rose (Mrs. Jack)
O'Laughlin, Russell
O'Rourke, A.E.
O'Rourke, Celia
O'Rourke, Frank
O'Rourke, Katie
O'Rourke, Myra
Oestrich, Ferdinand
Oestrich, Bertha (Mrs. Ferdinand)
Oestrich, Myrtle
Oestrich, Violet
Olive, C.D.
Omen, Bea

- P -
Palmer, Holger E.
Parks, Elizabeth (Mrs. Harding)
Parks, Milo S.
Paulson, Ida
Pederson, H.C.

Pehl, Ormonde
Peterson, Emma (Mrs. Walter)
Peterson, Walter
Peyton, Leona
Pfister, Dr. Herbert
Pithey, Agnes (Mrs. Fred)
Pithey, Fred
Pithey, Alice (later Schraeder)
Pithey, Harry (real name Royal)
Pithey, Mae
Pithey, Mary Belle (Mrs. Frank)
Polifka, Audrey (later Larson)
Polifka, Clifford
Polifka, Frank Herbert
Polifka, Mayme (Mrs. Frank)
Polifka, Helen A. (Mrs. John P.)
Polifka, John Peter
Polifka, LaVanche
Powell, Blanche
Propp, Agnes
Propp, Gustave A.
Propp, Lydia (Mrs. Gustave)
Propp, Metha
Propp, Ralph
Propp, Mrs. Ralph

- R -
Rabok, James
Rabok, Jeanette
Raguse, Fred "Fritz"
Ready, Elaine (later Kinker)
Ready, Emma (Mrs. John J.)
Ready, Ray
Ready, Esther (Mrs. Ray)
Ready, John

Reinhard, Diana
Remsberg, Marilyn
Remsberg, Oscar Zachariah
Remsberg, Stella (Mrs. Oscar)
Rice, Clara
Richardson, Amy (Mrs. John/Jack)
Richardson, John/Jack
Richardson, Charles
Richardson, James
Richardson, Ed
Richardson, Jennie (later Nelson)
Rieck, Martha
Riess, Mrs. Willard
Rising, Arthur
Rising, Katie (Mrs. Arthur)
Rixe, Luella
Roach, David
Roach, Ethel (Mrs. Frank)
Roach, Leland
Roach, Maurice
Roach, Winston
Roberts, Stanley
Rogahn, Herman
Rose, Daisy (Mrs. Merrill)
Rose, Merrill
Rose, Henry Stines "H.S"
Rose, Anna (Mrs. H.S.)
Rubish, E.G.
Runnie, Nels

- S -
Sanderson, Mrs. C.
Sargeant, Evva
Sargeant, Lenore
Sarmen, Idella
Schendel, Clara (Mrs. William)
Schendel, Will

Schmit, Lena (Mrs. Joe)
Schotte, Casper
Schotte, Mary (Mrs. Casper)
Scott, Lillie (Mrs. Winfield)
Seely, Dorothy
Seffens, Clayton "C.A."
Shaffer, Eugene
Shaffer, Hattie
Shaw, John
Shelstad, Alma
Shepherd, Grover G.
Shepherd, Helen (Mrs. Grover)
Shepherd, Gay G.
Shoup, A.H.
Shoup, A.E.
Simmons, Ernest
Simpson, Florence
Simpson, Hazel (Mrs. James)
Simpson, James
Skar, Beto
Sletvold, Lena
Sloan, Fay
Sloan, May
Solheim, Thelma
Solon, Earl
Solon, Mary (Mrs. Earl)
Solon, Francis
Starkey, Marie
Stearns, Joe
Stelton, Matilda (Mrs. William)
Stoddard, M.I.
Strobusch, Harvey
Strobusch, Lizzie

- T -

Tange, Stanley
Templeton, Leon
Thom, Pauline
Thomson, T.M., possibly Theodore
Thorson, Violet

Togstad, Melvin
Tressler, Mrs. G.
Tunney, Gene
Tunney, June
Tyler, Mary (Mrs. Toby)
Tyler, Toby

- U -

Ulrich, Clara (Mrs. Gustav)
Ulrich, Luella
Ulrich, Wilbert

- V -

Van Tassel, Mrs.
Vauer, Mrs.
Veitch, Lucille
Vetter, Rudolph
Viste, Lena
Vogel, Helen
Volkert, Percy L.
Vorwerk, Arthur
Voss, Ann (Mrs. Harry?)
Voss, Harry
Voss, Delmer
Voss, Ed
Voss, Elsie (possibly Mrs. Ed)
Voss, Tillie

- W -

Wahl, Amelia (Mrs. Carl)
Wahl, Emil
Waite, Jack
Waite, Bobbie (later Schakner)
Waite, Doris
Waite, Edgar
Waite, Blanche (Mrs. Edgar)
Waite, Elaine
Waite, Evadna
Waite, Fern
Waite, Grace (Mrs. Earl)
Waite, Jennie (Mrs. Thomas)
Waite, John
Waite, Lois

Waite, Robert Roy
Waite, Mrs. Robert Roy
Waite, Roger
Waite, Willie
Welton, Jameas
Western, Clara
Wheeler, Harry J.
Wheeler, Mrs. Milton
Whitaker, Zelta Marie
White, Clifford
Wilbrecht, Helen
Wilkinson, George
Wilkinson, Gus
Wittman, Dale
Wittman, Lois (later Tracy)
Wittman, Minnie (Mrs. Alois/Louie)
Wittman, Norman
Wittman, Orville
Woodward, Barbara Ann
Woodward, George
Woodward, Grace
Woodward, Merle
Worm, Fern
Wray, Dr. William Edgar
Wray, Gertrude (Mrs. William)
Wray, Dorothy

- Y, Z -

Young, Stella (Mrs. Robert)
ZumMallen, Herman

Fictional or Literary Characters Appearing
on the Tenney Quilt

The fictional characters on the quilt fall into four categories: Mother Goose rhyme characters, juvenile literature characters, literary characters, and a category I will call "other."

Mother Goose Characters:
Bo-Peep
Bobby Shaftoe
Boy Blue
Jack Horner
Jack
Jill
Jenny Daw
King Cole
King of Hearts
Queen of Hearts
Margery Daw
Miss Muffet
Mistress Mary
Peter Piper
Tommy Tucker
Tom Piper
Mother Goose
Tom Snooks
Bessie Brooks

I was familiar with all of the above Mother Goose characters except Tom Snooks and Bessie Brooks. Further research revealed that there was a lesser known Mother Goose rhyme (more popular in the UK than USA) that went like this:

As Tommy Snooks and Bessie Brooks
Were walking out on Sunday
Says Tommy Snooks to Bessie Brooks,
"Tomorrow will be Monday"

Juvenile Literature Literature Characters:
Cinderella
Rip Van Winkle
Tom Playfair

While we are all familiar with Cinderella and Mr. Van Winkle, I was initially perplexed by name *Tom Playfair*. As it turns out, the Tom Playfair Series of books was a series of Father Finn's 27 Catholic novels for young people. Some have described them as a Catholic version of Charles Dickens' stories, or even the Hardy Boys series. They were read by hundreds of thousands of young people at the turn of the century and could very well have been on the classroom reading list at the Tenney School, or perhaps at St. Gall's Catholic Church in Campbell. The stories have quaint language and always have a moral. Tom Playfair, the main character, is an unruly little boy when he is sent to St. Maure's boarding school, but he develops into a good Catholic young man and leader—while still maintaining his high spirited personality.

Literary Characters:

Annabelle Lee (American poetry): "Annabelle Lee" was a poem written by Edgar Allen Poe in 1849, 79 years prior to the Tenney Quilt. Poe wrote the poem about his wife after her death. The very interesting tidbit that you can impress your friends and relatives with is the fact that Poe married sweet Annabelle Lee when she was the tender age of 13. Life may have been a bit stressful for this young bride as, in the year 1842, she suffered an aneurysm or some sort of burst blood vessel and was an invalid until her death from Tuberculosis in 1847. During the last years of her life, as well as the years after, Poe drank and was a heavy drug user. The poem speaks about the death of his beautiful Annabelle.

Becky Sharp (British novel): Becky Sharp was the main character in William Makepeace Thackeray's *Vanity Fair*, first published in 1847, 81 years prior to the Tenney Quilt. Becky, of low social status, pursues her best friend Amelia's brother, Joseph Sedley, a wealthy man. She worms her way into their household with the purpose of snagging Joseph. Though he is attracted to dear Becky, he knows that his family would never approve of such a union with a person of such low social status. So Joseph does not respond favorably to Becky's advances. A frustrated Becky leaves the family and proceeds to climb—or rather *claw*—her way up to the upper class using her charm and beauty and whatever female tools she has available. Literary criticism of the novel is universal in claiming that *Vanity Fair* paints a bleak picture of the human condition in that none of its characters are good people. A movie was made in 1935—after the Tenney Quilt—based on this novel. Miriam Hopkins was nominated for an Academy Award for her portrayal of Becky Sharp. Becky Sharp was considered at that time one of the most famous literary characters of the time, so it is no surprise that her character may be known to the people of Tenney.

Ben Hur (American novel): *Ben Hur* is the fictional story of Judah ben-Hur, a Judean man who, after being betrayed by his friend Messala, is enslaved. He regains his freedom a bitter and revengeful man, but is redeemed after encountering Jesus Christ and witnessing His crucifixion. The original novel was written by General

Lew Wallace in 1880 (48 years prior to the Tenney Quilt). Up until the time the novel was published, Harriet Beecher Stowe's *Uncle Tom's Cabin* was American's best selling novel. *Ben Hur* took over this coveted spot until 1936 when *Gone With the Wind* was published. In 1912, the Sears and Roebuck catalog published one million copies of *Ben Hur* to sell for 39 cents each. This was the largest single year print edition in American history.

Don Quixote (Spanish novel): The novel *Don Quixote de la Mancha* was a novel by the Spanish author Miguel de Cervantes. It is generally considered to be the first novel, and the best book in Spanish. It was written in two parts, the first published in 1605 and the second in 1615, a year before Cervantes' death. The story covers the journeys of Don Quixote and his squire, Sancho Panza. He is a regular guy of low social standing who digs stories of errant knights. He digs them so much he decides to become one, traveling as an errant knight with his trusty horse around Spain, saving, protecting, and righting the wrongs of the world. He wants to save the world and his intentions are good, but often his adventures end of doing more damage than good. Cervantes uses his characters to preach moral messages because he felt all novels should serve that purpose.

Evangeline (American poetry): Evangeline is the main character in a poem written by U.S. poet Henry Wadsworth Longfellow, published in 1847 (81 years prior to the Tenney Quilt). The poem has to do with the expulsion of the French Acadians out of their homeland which is now known as Nova Scotia. Britain took over Acadia in 1713. In 1755, England deported native Acadians to various other places including Louisiana the east coast of the United States, Newfoundland, and in some cases, France and Quebec. The poem *Evangeline* describes the land of Acadia, its people, and their unfair and unjust separation from lost loved ones. The heroine Evangeline is separated from her beloved Gabriel and they both experience the agony of lovers separated. The story focuses on the beauty and strength of a woman's devotion, a woman who spends a lifetime in search of a lost love. The devastation of losing the love of her life drove Evangeline to insanity and eventually, death. The poem is based on the true story of Emmeline Labiche and her love, Louis Arceneaux, who were separated when the British invaded Nova Scotia.

Gabriel: Given that Evangeline is also included on the quilt, it is assumed that this name, Gabriel, refers to Evangeline's beloved Gabriel in the poem, *Evangeline*.

George Babbitt (American novel): George Babbitt is the primary character in Sinclair Lewis' novel, *Babbitt*, published in 1922 (only six years prior to the Tenney Quilt). George Babbitt is a real estate broker living in the fictional city, Zenith and married to Myra, with three children. He lives an unfulfilled and, well, boring life. He means well, but is basically a weak person. When his best friend Paul is imprisoned after shooting his wife and there is a strike in the town of Zenith, George escapes his drab life and runs off to Maine where he takes a mistress and wiles away the days partying, drinking, and carousing. Eventually the strike ends in Zenith, and the businessmen in the community form the Citizens League to work against the damn radicals who caused the strike in the first place. George Babbitt has, by this time, returned to Zenith. He refuses to join the Citizens League. But soon George's wife forgives him for all his transgressions, his heart softens, and his rebellious streak settles down. He joins the Citizens League and returns to his place in the community of Zenith. The novel is generally thought to be Sinclair Lewis' criticism of American business and American businessmen.

Gunga Din (British poetry): *Gunga Din* is a famous poem written by Joseph Rudyard Kipling (1865-1936) in 1892. It is a story of three British officers and best friends who are 19th century musketeers in India, their male-bonded trio threatened by a woman who is lusting after one of them. Gunga Din is the Indian water carrier of the regiment who longs to be a soldier himself.

Lady Macbeth (British drama): Lady Macbeth is both a literary character and a real person, upon whom the literary character is based. In the British drama, Lady Macbeth is loving to her husband, but at the same time quite wicked and overly ambitious. She would do anything in order to see her husband be king, so that she can also reap the benefits of his high social standing. She convinces her husband Macbeth to kill King Duncan, and then masterminds and orchestrates the killing, though Macbeth does the actual deed himself. Lady Macbeth frames the three palace guards by putting the victim's blood on their swords. Eventually Lady Macbeth's physical and mental condition deteriorates as her conscience gets the best of her, to the point where she commits suicide. She could no longer live with the guilt. The Lady Macbeth character has come to symbolize a wife who puses her husband to do harm through her own ambition. The real Lady Macbeth Bruoch lived from the years 1007 to 1060 and was the daughter of the prince of Scotland. In 1032, her father arranged for her marriage to Lord Macbeth, who would become the king of Scotland in 1040. She was only known as Lady Macbeth after that point. The play, *Macbeth*, is only loosely based on actual events.

Scrooge (British novel): Ebenezer Scrooge is the main character in Charles Dickens' *A Christmas Carol*, published in 1843 (85 years prior to the Tenney Quilt). Scrooge is an old and bitter man. He undergoes, however, a profound change of heart after being visited by three ghosts on Christmas Eve. Those ghosts are the Ghost of Christmas Past, the Ghost of Christmas Present, and the Ghost of Christmas Future. The ghosts show him that he needs to change his attitude toward his fellow man and in the end, Ebenezer Scrooge becomes a kind-hearted human being.

Silas Marner (British novel): Silas Marner is the main character and the name of the novel written by George Eliot (the pen name of writer Mary Ann Evans), and published in 1861. The setting is an English village in the early nineteenth century. Silas Marner was a weaver. He was a man who had earlier been wrongfully accused of a crime, and spent much of the rest of his life accumulating gold. As he collected and counted more, his life seemingly became emptier. His gold was one day stolen by the son of Squire Cass, a prominent man in town. Through a complex and interesting series of events, Silas finds himself with an adopted daughter, Eppie, who took the place of the missing gold in his life. It caused Silas' soul to soar and to bloom, as he loved the little girl more than he had loved his gold. The giral was actually the daughter of Godfrey, the brother of the man who stole Silas' gold, but this was a secret only Godfrey know. He and his new wife could have no children, and he grew to want Eppie for his own, but Eppie chose to stay with the aging Silas Marner, who had loved and cared for her. Godfrey eventually accepted this. *Silas Marner* teaches the values of honesty, kindness, and courage. As is true with her other novels, George Eliot featured the complex psychological lives of ordinary laborers in this novel.

Enock Arden (British poetry): Enoch Arden is the main character in a poem written by Alfred Lord Tennyson in 1864 (64 years prior to the Tenney Quilt), which is often called a "Victorian best-seller." Enoch Arden is married and has a family, but falls upon hard luck and takes to the seas as a sailor to rebuild his family's fortune. He is shipwrecked and finds himself alone on a desert island, and lives there for several years. His family presumes him dead. His wife eventually marries Enoch's best friend and is very happy and they prosper. Enoch Arden eventually makes his way back to his home town, and spies on his wife and her new family. Enoch decides not to reveal himself in order that his wife and family may continue their happy existence. He dies never having revealed his identity to his long lost family, after a lonely existence in a rented room in the same town. Enoch's landlady eventually figures out who he really is, but does not reveal it to his family until after Enoch's death. The term, "Enock Arden," also refers to a person who is presumed dead but is later found to be alive.

Maggie Tulliver (British novel): Maggie Tulliver is the main character in George Eliot's *The Mill on the Floss*, published in 1860 (68 years prior to the Tenney Quilt). It is considered a Victorian classic. Maggie is the daughter of a miller in England. She falls in love with Philip Wakem, the son of a local lawyer. A hitch in the romantic plan ensues when Maggie's father and Philip have a legal dispute, which resultssss in Mu. Tulliver's bankruptcy. Not long after her father's death, Maggie leaves the mill to live with her cousin, Lucy, and promptly has an affair with Lucy's husband. The underlying tensions in this novel are Maggie's own nature divided between moral responsibility and her passionate hunger for self-fulfillment.

Polyanna (British novel): *Polyanna* is the story of an orphaned girl who lives with her strict Aunt Polly. The novel was first published in 1913 (15 year s prior to the Tenney Quilt), and is often compared to *Anne of Green Gables.* It is a story written for young women. The young girl and her Aunt Polly develop trust in each other after facing many obstacles, a story of eternal optimism. The publication of this book spawned the formation of "Glad" clubs all over the country. I remember the 1960 movie based on this book, starring Hayley Mills. It was apparently a box office smash hit.

Other:

Santa Claus: No introduction needed. The big fella even found Tenney!

Wamba: This is an interesting and mysterious name choice for the Tenney Quilt. I think the mystery will remain. Seemingly the greatest use of this name would be for Wamba, a seventh century Spanish king who has several legends attached to his name. There is a statue of Wamba in Madrid. There was also a thoroughbred racing horse named Wamba in the early nineteenth century. And there are towns by the name of Wamba, in Texas (Texas' northeasternmost town, not far from Texarkana), and in the African country of Kenya. Take your pick. I think the most likely scenario is that some family in town had a dog named Wamba!

Folly: Though this seems that it certainly must refer to a particular character in a children's book or verse of the time, I can find no such evidence. We will have to revert to Merriam and Webster's definitions: "Lack of good sense or normal prudence and foresight, a foolish act or idea, or an often extravagant picturesque building erected to suit a fanciful taste."

Cecil and Elmo: Any help out there? I just don't know these guys.

Barney Google: Barney Google was the main character, with goo-goo-googly eyes" in a comic strip created by Billy DeBeck in 1919. It started out as a sports strip. Barney, half as tall as most of his supporting characters, enjoyed horse racing and prize fighting. In 1922, Barney was given the gift of a race horse named "Spark Plug," and that's when the comic strip really became popular. Spark Plug, or "Sparky" as he became known, was a race horse and his first race was anticipated by literally millions of newspaper readers. Spark Plug was such a star during the 1920s that children who enjoyed the comics often received the nickname "Sparky." A 1923 Billy Rose song was based on the Barney Google comic strip character. My favorite verse:

Barney Google, with the goo-goo-goo-ga-ly eyes
Barney Google had a wife three times his size
She stood Barney for divorce
Now he's living with his horse.

Sally Irene: This could be a real person, but is on a quilt square with other fictional names, which leads me to believe that it's a character in a book of the times. I have yet to find any significance to this name. The closest thing I can find is a movie, originally made in 1925, named "Sally, Irene and Mary," starring Joan Crawford. Sources are conflicting, however, as to the release date. Some say 1925; some say 1938. Obviously if it is the latter, it could not have been the inspiration for this name on the quilt. And besides, why didn't they include Mary?

Gene Tunney: This is an interesting mystery. Gene Tunney was the heavyweight boxing champion from 1926 to 1928, so was a popular sports figure in this time period. There was a major fight between Gene Tunney and the heavyweight champion Jack Dempsey in September, 1926, two years prior to the quilt. They fought during Philadelphia's sesquicentennial celebration, drawing 120,000 spectators. Dempsey was out of shape due to his playboy lifestyle and lost to Gene Tunney, who thus became the new heavyweight champion. There was a rematch in September, 1927, at Soldier Field in Chicago before 102,000 fans, plus 50,000 radio listeners. Tunney got the decision, so remained the champ. Radios had come to Tenney and there certainly would have been people in Tenney interested and listening to that fight on that day in 1927. Tunney defended his title only one more time, in July 1928, in New York—the precise time during which signatures were being collected for the Tenney Quilt. He retired a very wealthy man after that 1928 fight. Mr. Tunney stayed in the limelight, marrying a wealthy heiress and enjoying a successful business career. While it seems quite reasonable that the name embroidered on the Tenney Quilt indeed represented the boxer Gene Tunney, the mystery lies in the name that appears right next to it, "June Tunney." Gene Tunney's wife was Polly, and he didn't marry until after 1928, anyway. Census information shows no Gene or June Tunney anywhere near Tenney, Minnesota---can anybody out there help solve the mystery?

The Minnesota Quilt Project

The Tenney Quilt has enjoyed some recent publicity, being one of several quilts featured in a book entitled <u>Minnesota Quilts: Creating Connections With Our Past</u>, published by Voyageur Press in May, 2005. The quilt is part of the Minnesota Quilt Project, whose members traveled the state of Minnesota for twenty years documenting its quilts and their stories. The quilt is registered with this organization as No. KN007.

MINNESOTA QUILTS: CREATING CONNECTIONS WITH OUR PAST
A Treasury of Exceptional Quilts, Fascinating Quilters, and Their Stories...from the Minnesota Quilt Project
    Photography by Greg Winter and Lee Sandberg
    Text by the Minnesota Quilt Project
    Forward by Helen Kelley
    Voyageur Press, 2005
The Tenney Quilt is featured on page 105

Dating the Tenney Quilt

The Tenney Quilt had no label or signed date. In addition, no newspaper accounts or written documentation existed which refer to the quilt. Thus, determining the date the quilt was made necessitated an investigative process on my part. In a sense, dating a signature quilt such as this is infinitely easier than dating a plain decorative quilt. In most cases, it is an inexact science, piecing together clues such as the fabrics used in the quilt, the colors used, construction details, pattern, and size. And of course any documentation, including oral history, is extremely valuable to dating a quilt.

In the case of the Tenney Quilt, the clues pointing to the year 1928 were the 530 names embroidered on the quilt. Through a painstaking process of researching each of the 530 names in order to find clues—birth dates, marriage dates, death dates—I was gradually able to zero in on a date that would make sense.

Listed below are some of the names on the Tenney Quilt which provided the key to unlocking 1928 as the year the quilt was made—in the order in which I discovered them.

Audrey Polifka, my grandmother, married A.N. Larson on September 28, 1930, and took the last name "Larson" at that time. Given that her name on this quilt is her maiden name, Audrey *Polifka*, this dates the quilt to some time before September 28, 1930.

Mary Belle Pithey was married September 27, 1927, the date on which her name changed from Mary Belle Berry to Mary Belle Pithey. Given that her name is listed as Mary Belle *Pithey* on the quilt, her married name, we know that the quilt was made sometime after her September 27, 1927 marriage. So just from these two names, we have narrowed the date down to a three-year period between September, 1927 and September, 1930.

Muriel Lee Edner. Muriel Lee was born December 30, 1927. Her name appearing on this quilt indicates, obviously, that the quilt was made sometime after her birth date. So we have now further narrowed the date to a 33-month period between December, 1927, (Muriel Lee Edner's birth date) and September, 1930 (Audrey Larson's marriage date).

Ann Max. Ann Max was married to Oscar Wood on January 29, 1929, and took the last name *Wood* at that time. Given that her last name appears as her maiden name, Ann *Max*, on the quilt, we now know that the quilt was made sometime before January 29, 1929. We have now narrowed the date to a 24-month period between December, 1927 (Muriel Lee Edner's birth) and January, 1929 (Ann Max's wedding date).

Hattie Shaffer. Through the Tenney news in the Breckenridge paper of 1928, I learned that Hattie Richardson and Gene Shaffer were married June 30, 1928. Hattie's name appears on the quilt as Hattie *Shaffer*, her married name, thus dating the quilt to sometime after this date. The quilt date is now narrowed to a seven-month period between June, 1928 (Hattie's married date) and January, 1929 (Ann Max's marriage date).

Delmer Voss. Delmer was born August 23, 1928. Since his name appears on the quilt, we know the quilt was made after his birth.

So the gap has been narrowed to a five-month time period between the end of

August, 1928 and the end of January, 1929. This is as narrow as I have been able to make the gap, indicating that the names for the Tenney Quilt were collected in the late summer, fall, and early winter of 1928. Using this technique to find a specific time period in which the quilt was made does not necessarily mean that the quilt was actually constructed during this narrow period of time. But it does clearly represent the period of time in which the names were *collected*. In the case of the Tenney Quilt, once the squares were embroidered and sewn together, the quilt was sent to Dayton's Department Store in downtown Minneapolis to be stitched. This I consider to be a bit unusual for a fundraising quilt of the time, since there would have been a cost involved in having it machine-stitched by an outside party as opposed to getting together as a group of women and hand-stitching. I am guessing that the quilt would have been sent to Dayton's sometime during the late winter of 1928-29, and perhaps returned to the Tenney women by the summer or fall of 1929, for whatever activities or events designed for the purpose of auctioning or raffling off the quilt.

Note: Using this method to date the quilt worked well for the time period in question (the 1920s), but clearly would not work in the present day and age, when young women do not necessarily change their last names when they marry.

Works Cited

Bingham, M. (1989). Keeping At It: Minnesota Women. In C. E. Clark, *Minnesota in a Century of Change* (pp. 433-472). Minneapolis: Minnesota Historical Society Press.

Blegen, T. C. (1938). *Building Minnesota*. Boston: D.C. Heath.

Conzen, K. (2003). *Germans in Minnesota*. Minneapolis: Minnesota Historical Society Press.

Dumenil, L. (1995). *The Modern Temper: American Culture and Society in the 1920s*. New York: Hill and Wang.

Erickson, T. M. (1971). *Campbell's Community History*. Wahpeton, North Dakota: Globe-Gazette Printing Company.

Felder, D. G. (1997). *A Century of Women*. Seacaucus, NJ: Birch Lane Press.

Gazette Publications. (1968). Breckenridge Gazette. *Wilkin County 1968 Centennial Souvenir Edition* . Breckenridge-Wahpeton, Minnesota, U.S.A.: Gazette Publications.

Gulliford, A. (1984). *America's Country Schools*. Washington, DC: Preservation Press.

Gwynn, D. (2007). *A&P*. Retrieved September 4, 2007, from Grocerteria. com: www.grocerteria.com

Health Partners Inc. (2004). *Arthur B. Ancker Memorial School of Nursing: Timeline*. Retrieved August 27, 2007, from Regions Hospital: www. regionshospital.com

Health Partners Inc. (2004). *Our History*. Retrieved August 26, 2007, from Regions Hospital: www.regionshospital.com

Hurley, W. T. (2004, January 25). *Fergus Falls Photo Page: Fergus Falls Regional Treatment Center: History*. Retrieved August 27, 2007, from Fergus Photos: www.fergusphotos.com

Joseph, J. (2001). *Warning: When I Am Old I Shall Wear Purple*. London: Souvenir Press.

Kane, L. M. (1983). *Twin Cities: A Pictorial History of St. Paul and Minneapolis*. St. Paul: Minnesota Historical Society Press.

Kellogg NA Co. (2007). *Kellogg in the 1920s*. Retrieved September 4,

2007, from Kellogg's: www2.kelloggs.com

Kirocofe, R. (1993). *The American Quilt: A History of Cloth and Comfort 1750-1950.* New York: Clarkson Potter.

Kron, G. (1937). *History of Wilkin County Minnesota 1872 to 1937.* Breckenridge, MN: Self.

Lasansky, J. *In the Heart of Pennsylvania: 19th and 20th Century Quiltmaking Traditions.* Lewisburg, PA: Union County Historical Society Oral Traditions Project.

Marx Atkins, J. (1984). *Shared Threads.* New York: Viking Studio Books.

Miller, D. R. (1998). *1926 Events.* Retrieved September 4, 2007, from World History Timelines: www.din-timelines.com

MN State Univ Moorhead. (2007). *MSUM History.* Retrieved August 13, 2007, from Minnesota State University Moorhead: www.mnstate.edu

Monti, M. J. (2007, March 5). *Honeywell.* Retrieved July 26, 2007, from The Honeywell/ALlied Signal Retirees: www.hon-area.org

Murray, S. N. (1967). *The Valley Comes of Age.* Fargo: Dakota Institute for Regional Studies.

Nickel, L. a. (1984). *above+/charles-and-bertha-berry.html.* Retrieved August 19, 2007, from Old Timers USA: www.old-timers-usa.com

Parker, R. (1989). *The Subversive Stitch: Embroidery and the Making of the Feminine.* London: Routledge Press.

Premium Wear, Inc. (2006). Retrieved July 29, 2007, from Funding Universe: www.fundinguniverse.com

Regents of Univ of MN. (2006, December 5). *A Brief History.* Retrieved August 27, 2007, from University of Minnesota, Morris: www.morris.umn.edu/about

Rippley, L. (1989). *Of German Ways.* New York: Harper Collins.

Rowbotham, S. (1997). *A Century of Women: A History of Women in Britain and the United States.* New York: Viking Press.

Royal Neighbors of America. (2007). *Our Legacy.* Retrieved August 26, 2007, from Royal Neighbors of America: www.royalneighbors.org/About-RNA/History-of-RNA.aspx

Schwinn, J. A. (1984). Family History: Minto-Waite-Andersen. Self.

Sivulka, J. (1998). *Soap, Sex and Advertising*. Belmont, CA: Wadsworth.

Vaughan, R. (2002-2003). *Minnesota Women and Work Timeline: 1911-1934*. Retrieved July 29, 2007, from Minnesota Women and Work Oral History Collection: www.minnesotawomenwork.org

Wikimedia Foundation. (2007, July 23). *1928 in Film*. Retrieved August 26, 2007, from Wikipedia: www.wikipedia.org/wiki/1928_in_film

Wikimedia Foundation Inc. (2007, August 28). *Montgomery Ward*. Retrieved August 26, 2007, from Wikipedia: www.wikipedia.org

Wilkin County Historical Society. (1977). *Wilkin County Family History Book*. Dallas, TX: Taylor Publishing Company.

LaVergne, TN USA
14 February 2011
216529LV00001B/6/A